"As the historian explains why the winning side triumphed, he naturally tends to identify the victor with the most cherished values of the society in which he lives. . . . In American society there are three such values to which historians give adherence: All are convinced that it is a desirable and necessary thing to preserve the American Union; all believe that Negro slavery is an evil; and all profess a faith in democratic government.

"It is not the truth of these beliefs but their juxta-position which causes the great confusion about the Civil War. Historians, recognizing that Lincoln's government was fighting for the preservation of the Union and for the freedom of the slaves, attribute to it also the third great positive value, the defense of democracy. Such a view is a distortion of the facts . . . the Confederacy, not the Union, represented the democratic forces in American life.

"The democratic tendencies of the Confederacy were all too plainly reflected in its army. Accustomed to regarding themselves as the equals of any men in the world, the Southerners never took kindly to regimented life. Even their appearance showed that they considered themselves individualistic citizens who were temporarily assisting their country. One astonished Englishman . . . gasped: 'Anything less like the received notion, at home, of how a soldier should look . . . never met my eye.' "

—DAVID DONALD

Edited by DAVID DONALD

WHY
THE NORTH WON
THE CIVIL WAR

Essays by
RICHARD N. CURRENT
T. HARRY WILLIAMS
NORMAN A. GRAEBNER
DAVID DONALD
DAVID M. POTTER

With a Foreword by U. S. GRANT III

COLLIER BOOKS
Macmillan Publishing Company
NEW YORK
COLLIER MACMILLAN PUBLISHERS
LONDON

FIRST COLLIER BOOKS EDITION 1962

35   34   33   32

This Collier Books edition is published by arrangement with Louisiana State University Press.

Macmillan Publishing Company
866 Third Avenue, New York, N.Y. 10022
Collier Macmillan Canada, Inc.

ISBN 0-02-031660-7

Macmillan books are available at special discounts for bulk purchases for sales promotions, premiums, fund-raising, or educational use. For details, contact:

Special Sales Director
Macmillan Publishing Company
866 Third Avenue
New York, N.Y. 10022

Printed in the United States of America

Foreword

THIS BOOK makes a very real and important contribution to the appropriate observance of the War's Centennial and to a better understanding of its history. Each article is by a scholar and a specialist in his subject, and deals with an individual disadvantage under which the Confederacy labored and which prevented its ultimate success. Indeed, the title of the publication might better have been *Why the South Lost the Civil War*. But this is a minor distinction like Emerson's difference of the sea seen from the shore and the shore seen from the sea.

Each of the articles here assembled is an authoritative discussion of one of the factors that militated against the Confederacy's final victory. Moreover, these factors, presented from the overall point of view, too generally have been inadequately stressed or even entirely overlooked by many histories of the War. In now bringing these factors to public attention and giving them their proper emphasis lies the importance of this book. Even many "Civil War buffs" may be apprized of facts of which they have heretofore been unaware or to which they have given little thought.

As a footnote to Dr. Williams' excellent article on the military leadership of the North and South, it may be of interest that, on his trip around the world, General Grant said to Mr. John Russell Young: "If the Vicksburg campaign meant anything, in a military point of view, it was that there are no fixed laws of war which are not subject to the conditions of the country, the climate, and the habits of the people. The laws of successful war in one generation would insure defeat in another." And again: "Some of our generals failed because they worked out everything by rule. They knew what Frederick did at one place and Napoleon at another. They were always thinking about what Napoleon would do. Unfortunately for their plans, the rebels would be thinking about something

5

else. I don't underrate the value of military knowledge, but if men make war in slavish observances of rules, they will fail. No rules will apply to conditions of war as different as those which exist in Europe and America. Consequently, while our generals were working out problems of an ideal character, problems that would have looked well on a blackboard, practical facts were neglected. To that extent I consider remembrances of old campaigns a disadvantage. Even Napoleon showed that, for my impression is that his first success came because he made war in his own way."

Inevitably, the articles are special pleas and marshal the evidence in favor of their case. Naturally they do not give much attention to the like disadvantages and difficulties which the North had to overcome, but these are well summarized by the two outstanding English writers on the War, Colonel G. F. R. Henderson in his *Stonewall Jackson and the American Civil War* and Colonel J. F. C. Fuller in his *The Generalship of Ulysses S. Grant*, and which led the latter to write: "The outstanding marvel is that the North ever won."

However, although differences of opinion on military and economic phases and personalities of the War will persist, with the passage of a hundred years such differences of opinion have become academic, and we can well focus our attention on the heroism and self-sacrifice for the cause they thought right shown during those years by Americans on both sides, and take satisfaction in Sir Winston Churchill's summary: "Thus ended the great American Civil War, which must upon the whole be considered the noblest and least avoidable of all the great mass-conflicts of which till then there was record."

As Americans we can all today take pride in the fact that the bitter struggle did end with a reunited country for which the sons of those who fought one another so valiantly have since fought shoulder to shoulder in four foreign wars.

U. S. GRANT III
Major General, U.S.A., Ret'd

Editor's Preface

"THEY NEVER whipped us, Sir, unless they were four to one. If we had had anything like a fair chance, or less disparity of numbers, we should have won our cause and established our independence." This was one Virginian's pithy verdict of the outcome of the Civil War.

The general soul-searching in which many Southerners indulged after Appomattox brought forth other varied explanations of the catastrophe. Some were long-winded and intricate, such as Colonel Robert Tansill's *A Free And Impartial Exposition of the Causes Which Led to the Failure of the Confederate States to Establish Their Independence,* which itemized no fewer than thirteen causes, ranging from excessive "reliance upon foreign recognition and succors" to the election of military officers, "a policy subversive of good order, military discipline and efficiency." Others were more sober and compact, such as "The Causes of the Failure of Southern Independence," by Robert Garlick Hill Kean, former head of the Confederate Bureau of War. Kean listed seven principal reasons for the collapse of the Confederacy, including a bankrupt treasury, want of men, lack of subsistence, incompetency of military men, want of transport, recruiting difficulties, and desertion by slaves.

Later historians continued the argument which contemporaries thus began. Many writers sided with Albert Bushnell Hart, who cogently argued in 1891 that the South was overwhelmed by Northern preponderance in men and resources. Others, like James Ford Rhodes, disagreed, contending that Northern numerical superiority was "none too great" for an offensive war, and found elsewhere the key to Southern defeat.

Relatively few historians have devoted much attention specifically to the sources of Northern strength during the Civil War. Not until the recent publication of Allan Nevins' *The War for the Union: The Improvised War,*

1861–1862 did anyone trouble to list in tabular form the comparative resources of the two sections in 1860. Generations of Lincoln biographers, however, attributed Union victory to the superior political leadership of the North; Rhodes, for example, declared flatly: "The preponderating asset of the North proved to be Lincoln." Such students of military history as J. F. C. Fuller, B. H. Liddel Hart, Kenneth P. Williams, and T. Harry Williams stressed the excellence of Northern military leadership. J. R. Soley contended that the Northern blockade was the chief reason for Southern defeat. E. D. Adams, Frank L. Owsley, and Jay Monaghan maintained that Europe's failure to intervene, whether attributable to superior Union diplomacy or to selfish European economic and political considerations, was of decisive importance in securing Northern victory.

Many more historians have analyzed the weaknesses of the Confederacy. Among those who stressed the economic weaknesses of the South, Charles W. Ramsdell singled out finances as "the greatest single weakness of the Confederacy," Robert C. Black, III, pointed out the failure of the Confederate transportation system, and Frank Vandiver blamed Southern inability to "evolve a command or logistical system adequate to the job at hand." Among the numerous critics of the Confederacy's political leadership, Burton J. Hendrick and Clifford Dowdey are perhaps the most convincing.

Other writers have documented the internal dissensions of the Confederacy. Georgia Lee Tatum stressed the role of desertion and disloyalty in weakening the South, and Frank L. Owsley declared that the tombstone of the Confederacy should bear the inscription: "Died of State Rights." Both Edward Channing and Charles H. Wesley attributed Southern failure to the loss of the will to fight, and Lawrence Henry Gipson maintained that the Southern people, "questioning the justification of secession and still more uncertain as to the end in view," were "distracted unto desperation by internal strife [and were] in need of a great leader." Clement Eaton endorsed a contemporary verdict that the Confederacy lost "because there was no Wisdom in Congress and no Public Virtue among the People." Bell Irvin Wiley felt that the South failed in "flexibility, public information, harmony, morale and leadership."

With so many theories already adduced to explain the collapse of the Confederacy, the authors of the present volume did not set out to invent new explanations for Northern victory. Invited to participate in a conference on this theme at Gettysburg College in November, 1958, each of the five undertook as his assignment the re-examination of one of the familiar interpretations of the outcome of the Civil War. In so doing, they have illustrated the advantages of taking new thought about old subjects. The essays in this book emerged from their contributions to that conference.

Applying contemporary economic theory to an analysis of the economic resources of the two regions, Professor Richard N. Current, of the University of Wisconsin, throws new light on the war-making potential of the North and South. Professor T. Harry Williams, of Louisiana State University, demonstrates that military history has a new significance when interpreted in relation to the main currents of intellectual and social history. Professor Norman A. Graebner, of the University of Illinois, shows how Civil War diplomacy should be reevaluated in terms of the broad European diplomatic tradition. Drawing upon the insights political science offers historians, Professor David M. Potter, of Yale University, suggests the hitherto heretical idea that the North benefited by the presence of two well-organized political parties. My essay indicates that defects in the social and institutional structure of the Confederacy should be considered.

In their reinvestigations of the causes of Southern defeat, the five authors of this book have by no means found themselves in unanimous agreement. Perhaps the basic argument is between Current, who holds that the North's "overwhelming preponderance in most sources of economic power" made Southern defeat "all but inevitable," and the other writers, who believe that, had the Confederacy better managed its resources, Southern independence might have been won. Williams, Graebner, Potter, and I are not, however, agreed as to the source of Confederate weakness. Williams blames Southern generalship, and Graebner tends to agree, stressing that Europe could not intervene "until the South had demonstrated the power to establish and maintain its independence." Potter, on the other hand, accuses Southern political leaders, while I have found the basic fault in too great a respect for democratic liberties in the Confederacy.

The five writers differ also in their allocation of personal responsibility for Northern victory. Williams and I have arrived at adverse verdicts upon Jefferson Davis and his administration, and Potter declares boldly: "If the Union and the Confederacy had exchanged presidents with one another, the Confederacy might have won its independence." But Current concludes: "It is hard to believe, and impossible to prove, that the Southerners did a worse job with economic affairs than Northerners would have done in the same circumstances," and Graebner maintains that neither the deficiencies of the Confederate foreign service nor the skill of Union diplomats, but "the realities of power" determined Europe's decision not to intervene.

All these disagreements, it hardly needs adding, are of an entirely good-natured sort, for none of the five authors is committed to a monolithic scheme of causation and none is blind to the cogent considerations advanced by his colleagues. We hope that these essays, written from five different points of view, will not so much contradict as complement each other. If they do nothing more than demonstrate how complex the problem of historical causation is and how wary writers must be of oversimplification, they will have served their purpose.

All five of us wish to express our gratitude to the officials of Gettysburg College, especially to President Willard S. Paul, Professor Robert Bloom, and Mr. Raymond S. Davis, who did so much to make our conference a successful one. These essays have all been improved by the criticisms of other scholars who participated in the conference: J. Cutler Andrews; Clifford Dowdey; John Hope Franklin; Fletcher M. Green; Warren W. Hassler, Jr.; William B. Hesseltine; David C. Mearns; and Roy F. Nichols. It is unfortunately not possible to convey our deepest appreciation to the original organizer of the Gettysburg College Civil War conferences, for Professor Robert Fortenbaugh died while this book was being prepared for publication.

DAVID DONALD

Princeton University

Contents

God and the Strongest Battalions

Richard N. Current

WHEN WAR BEGAN in 1861, the statistics from the latest federal census decidedly favored the twenty-three states remaining in the Union as against the eleven that had withdrawn from it. In population the North had an advantage of almost five to two, and this advantage appears even greater if the slaves (more than one-third of the Southern people) are counted as somewhat less than the same number of freemen. In wealth and capacity to produce, the North held a still greater edge: in value of real and personal property, more than three to one (even with the inclusion of $2 billion for the slave property of the South); in capital of incorporated banks, more than four to one; in value of products annually manufactured, more than ten to one. The seceded states probably had a much less than proportional share of the national income. Besides, they contained only about a third of the total railroad mileage and practically none of the registered shipping. Though these comparisons are incomplete and inexact, they will serve to illustrate the point that the Union went to war with an overwhelming preponderance in most sources of economic power.

If wars are won by riches, there can be no question why the North eventually prevailed. The only question will be: How did the South manage to stave off defeat so long? Or perhaps the question ought to be: Why did the South even risk a war in which she was all but beaten before the first shot was fired?

Indeed, this last question occurred to at least a few Southerners during the secession winter. For example, the editor of the Lynchburg *Virginian* wrote: "Dependent upon Europe and the North for almost every yard of cloth, and every coat and boot and hat that we wear, for our axes, scythes, tubs, and buckets, in short, for every-

15

thing except our bread and meat, it must occur to the
South that if our relations with the North are ever severed,
—and how soon they may be none can know; may God
forbid it long!—we should, in all the South, not be able
to clothe ourselves; we could not fill our firesides, plough
our fields, nor mow our meadows; in fact, we should be
reduced to a state more abject than we are willing to look
at even prospectively. And yet, all of these things staring
us in the face, we shut our eyes and go in blindfold." Of
course, the view of the Lynchburg *Virginian* was not the
prevailing attitude of Southerners at that time. If it had
been, most likely there would have been no war.

Nor was this the opinion of most leading Southerners
afterwards, when the war had been lost and they were
casting about for reasons why it had been. These men
refused to adopt the handy and easy rationalization that
the North simply had been too much and too many for the
South. These men could not very well accept such an
explanation, for it would have convicted them of blind-
ness, stupidity, or even worse in going into a conflict they
could not hope to win. In his memoirs General Joseph E.
Johnston defended his fellow Southerners against such a
possible charge. "That people," he wrote, "was not guilty
of the high crime of undertaking a war without the means
of waging it successfully."

As Johnston looked back, it seemed to him that the
Confederacy had possessed "ample means." Other Southerners agreed with him. General P. G. T. Beauregard, for
one, declared that "no people ever warred for independence with more relative advantages than the Confederacy;
and if, as a military question, they must have failed, then
no country must aim at freedom by means of war." The
outcome was not to be explained, Beauregard insisted, by
"mere material contrast" between the North and the
South. So, too, the Richmond journalist and historian
Edward A. Pollard maintained that "something more than
numbers makes armies" and that "against the vast superiority of the North in material resources," the South had
"a set-off in certain advantages."

Among these presumed advantages of the South, the first was psychological. Her people, fighting as they did for the high ideal of independence, for the protection of their very homes, were moved by a "superiour animation," a more determined spirit than the enemy could attain. The second point in the South's favor was geographic. She possessed rivers, swamps, and mountains that were "equivalent to successive lines of fortification"; she had the "immense advantage of the interior lines"; and, besides all this, she was favored with "one single advantage" which, alone, "should have been decisive of the contest." "That advantage was *space*." Even some economic aspects favored the South: At the beginning of the war it was a "remarkable fact" that "the South was richer than the North in all the *necessaries* of life," producing as she did more corn and livestock per person. The fourth and most important item might be viewed as either economic or diplomatic. This was cotton—a magic word, a magic staple, which theoretically ought to have done wonders for the Confederacy.

If statistics were on the side of the North, history seemed to be on the side of the South. In previous struggles for liberty the Dutch had beaten the Spaniards, the Russians had repelled the French, and the Americans had won out over the British against odds as bad or worse than those the Southerners faced in 1861. "In an intelligent view of the precedents of history," Pollard concluded, "it might safely [have been] predicted that the South . . . would be victor in the contest, however unequally matched in men and the materials of war, *unless the management of her affairs should become insane, or her people lose the virtue of endurance*."

Possibly, then, the Confederacy at last succumbed not because of any economic handicap but because of a loss of virtue, that is, of morale or fighting spirit. This, indeed, is the view of Charles H. Wesley, who discounts the "customary" explanation of the collapse of the Confederacy as due to Northern economic preponderance, and who repudiates the "astonishing conclusion that we must all be amazed that the Confederacy was able to continue the contest for so long a period." According to Wesley, the "psychological factors which entered into the disruption of Southern morale and the inherent political weaknesses of the Confederacy were fundamental" in bringing about the final collapse. But other writers deny that a failure of will was the prime cause of defeat. They point to the fact that Southerners sacrificed far more for the Lost Cause than the Revolutionary patriots had sacrificed for victory over England.

If the defeat was not due to a loss of will to win, then perhaps it was caused by bad management, by human errors, by failures of statesmanship. Certainly the carping Pollard thought so. His book is replete with contemptuous references to the policies of the Jefferson Davis government—with such phrases as "silly prospects," "a new delusion," "silly declamation," "puerile argument," "feeble and mismanaged efforts," "a policy of blunders," "silly devices," and "childish expedients." Pollard, of course, enjoyed the privilege of the second guess. Other similarly privileged critics of the Davis government, while not always agreeing with Pollard in detail, concurred with him in the general proposition that the Confederacy had fallen because of mistakes in the use of its resources and not because of a lack of sufficient resources to begin with.

In economic policy the chief errors commonly attributed to the Confederate government are these: its failure to exploit cotton promptly as a basis for foreign credit; its unwillingness to tax its people and its reliance, instead, on issues of paper money in the form of treasury notes; its impressment, or seizure at arbitrary prices, of the goods of its citizens; and its lack of thoroughness in the promotion of manufacturers and in the control of transportation, especially by railroad. A brief re-examination of these matters may throw light on the question of whether the Confederacy was more handicapped by human or by material shortcomings.

In cotton, the South had a cash crop of great value, and yet, in the midst of war, Southerners reduced their planting, burned some of the bales they had on hand, and discouraged shipments abroad. "Instead of making the best use of this resource," B. J. Hendrick observes, "the Davis government deliberately did all in its power to make it useless." At first glance the policy appears downright insane.

Surely there were alternatives, and in fact the Vice-President of the Confederacy, Alexander H. Stephens, proposed a different course during the war. Take two million bales from the 1860 and another two million from the 1861 crop, Stephens recommended. Pay for these with $100 million in government bonds. Buy fifty ironclad steamers to carry the cotton safely to Europe. Store it there until the price rises to fifty cents a pound, then sell it. Thus, Stephens thought, the Confederacy could net a profit of $800 million! Afterwards General Johnston was positive that this plan, if promptly put into effect, would have won the war. The cotton money, Johnston averred, would have procured arms for half a million men, who could have been ready and in the field by the time the very first battle was fought. The first battle, he implied, might well have been the last. In any event, "the Confederate treasury would have been much richer than that of the United States," and the South would have had the means of eventual success.

That the Confederacy failed to seize this splendid and obvious opportunity during the first year of the war—before the blockade had become too tight—must prove the stupidity if not the insanity of government leaders, of President Davis and his Secretary of the Treasury, Christopher G. Memminger. So it afterward seemed to historian Pollard, who berated Memminger for not having purchased cotton and sent it abroad while he had the chance. Pollard said Memminger had dismissed the Stephens plan as "soup-house legislation," as a scheme of government relief for cotton planters. But historian Pollard forgot a great deal that journalist Pollard had said during the war. Actually, it was Pollard's Richmond *Examiner* which had denounced Stephens for proposing "soup-house legislation." Afterwards, having reversed himself, Pollard put his own words into the mouth of poor Memminger!

The truth is that neither Davis nor Memminger had foisted upon the South the idea of withholding cotton. When the war began, not only these two men but practically all Southern leaders believed that cotton—or rather the lack of it—would win the war for the South. On the Southern staple Great Britain presumably depended for its prosperity, and so did France, and so too did the United States. Without cotton, Great Britain and France would face economic prostration, and to avert this they would have to come to the Confederacy's aid. Without cotton, the United States would suffer the closing of its textile mills and, more important, would have no export crop sufficient for obtaining indispensable foreign exchange. If the notions about "King Cotton" were delusions, they were not the private dreams of Memminger or Davis.

In the light of the times, these ideas were not quite so crazy as they seem in retrospect. True, the cotton shortage failed to accomplish what Southerners had expected it to do. Yet it did create a serious problem for the North, the problem of finding means of payment for necessary imports. Unfortunately for Southern hopes, the North was able to make up for her lack of cotton shipments by means of increased exports of wheat. Unfortunately, also, there were British economic interests that ran counter to the British interest in continued cotton shipments from the South, as Frank L. Owsley had demonstrated.

The Stephens-Johnston-Pollard view regarding cotton exports was at least as visionary as the King Cotton theory itself. There simply was not so much cotton available in 1861 as Stephens estimated: there were not two million bales left over from the 1860 crop, but only a few hundred thousand. Then, too, it is doubtful whether many owners of this cotton would have given it up in return for Confederate bonds. Even if enough money were obtained, the fifty ironclads probably could not have been purchased, and without them the South did not have enough shipping to send the cotton overseas. "Finally," Rembert

W. Patrick concludes, "the idea . . . that with four million bales in storage the price of cotton would have risen to fifty cents a pound, was fanciful."

Granting that Stephens' gigantic cotton-export scheme was not feasible in 1861, there remains the question whether *something* could not have been accomplished by a more prompt and vigorous export policy than was adopted. Whether or not Davis and Memminger should have done more than they did to base financing upon cotton, the fact is that they did more than their critics have credited them with doing. The cotton embargo, it must be remembered, was not the work of the Davis administration or of the Confederate Congress. It was the work of state and local officials and private groups, who had the backing of an almost unanimous public opinion. It did not have the official support of Memminger and Davis, who used their influence to prevent Congress from passing an embargo act, and who encouraged shipments of cotton in so far as vessels were available. Almost from the outset, the Confederate government sought to obtain cotton by purchase or by produce loan, keeping some of it at home as a basis of credit for the purchase of foreign supplies, and sending the rest abroad. The fiasco of the Erlanger loan resulted from an attempt to use cotton for bolstering the foreign credit of the Confederacy. Not until the third year of the war, however, did the government take complete control of cotton exports and push them with determination. If this program had been undertaken earlier, probably Confederate finances could have been made much stronger than they actually became.

Certainly, Confederate financing was much less sound and less successful than Union financing. Of the Confederacy's income, to October 1864, almost 60 per cent was derived from the issue of paper money, about 30 per cent from the sale of bonds, and less than 5 per cent from taxation (the remaining 5 per cent arising from miscellaneous sources). Of the Union's income, by contrast, 13 per cent was raised by paper money, 62 per cent by bonds, and 21 per cent by taxes (and 4 per cent by other means). Thus the Confederacy relied much more upon government notes and much less upon taxation and borrowing than the Union did. Exactly how much paper money was afloat in the wartime South, nobobdy knows for sure. "Even if we knew the successive amounts of Confederate treasury notes in the hands of the public during the war," John C. Schwab remarks, "this would signify little, as they formed but a part of the currency; the State, municipal, bank, corporate, and individual notes formed the other, and . . . no inconsiderable part." The economist Eugene M. Lerner estimates that the stock of money in the South increased approximately eleven fold in the three years from January, 1861, to January, 1864. In any case, the prices of gold and other commodities were multiplied by much more than eleven. The price of gold, in Confederate dollars, rose eventually to sixty-one (in United States greenbacks it never rose even as high as three). The general price level, in Confederate dollars, soared to ninety or a hundred times its original level. The Confederacy suffered the worst inflation that Americans had known since the Revolutionary War.

In its effort to escape the evils of inflation the Confederate government but compounded them. The Funding Act of 1864, designed to force the exchange of treasury notes for bonds by threatening a partial repudiation of the notes, only speeded the loss in value of the currency. The impressment of government supplies, at less than the inflated market price, caused suppliers to withhold their goods and thus lessened the available amount. Unwittingly, the government defeated its own purposes. "The army suffered from want of food," as Schwab has observed, "though in the country at large there was no serious lack of it."

To the later critics of the Davis government it was perfectly obvious that the government should have taxed and taxed and borrowed and borrowed, rather than relying so heavily on the printing of batch after batch of treasury notes. These critics blamed Secretary Memminger, and some historians still blame him (Owsley refers to him as the "measly" Memminger). In truth, however, Memminger was just as well aware of the dangers of inflation as any of his denouncers. They were to have hindsight; he had at least a degree of foresight. But there was little he could do, especially since he lacked the force of personality to carry the Congress with him. As for taxes, he favored them, but at the start of the war he had no going machinery of tax collection to work with, and he was dealing with people who had even more than the typical American's resistance to taxation. Besides, cash was comparatively scarce in the Confederacy. The Secretary and the Congress had little choice but to resort to the 1861 requisition upon the states, which the states raised almost entirely by borrowing instead of taxing. As for issuing bonds to sop up the excess currency, Memminger favored that too, but the plain fact was that the people would not or could not buy the bonds in sufficient quantities. Hence his recommendation of the funding scheme to force the sale of bonds—a scheme that Congress carried even farther than he had intended.

There can be no doubt that the government's fiscal policies failed in their main object, namely, to transfer goods efficiently from private to public hands. There is considerable doubt, however, whether Davis or Memminger or any individual was to blame. There also is doubt whether the paper money issues, alone, accounted for the extent of inflation in the South. Actually, the price rise was uneven, and the prices that rose the most were those of goods in short supply, such as leather, wool, coffee, salt, tea, and drugs. So the actual scarcity of some items, as well as the overabundance of money, seems to have been responsible for soaring prices. Moreover, the flight from the currency, at least during the last couple of years of the war, must have been due in part to a growing popular skepticism as to the chances of the Confederacy's ever winning the war and making good on its promises to pay.

By interfering with the free market, the Davis government unintentionally discouraged production, both agricultural and industrial. At the same time the government did not interfere enough by means of positive measures to make the most of manufacturing possibilities. "The failure of the Confederacy, though predictable from the start," Ella Lonn writes, "was immediately attributable to errors of judgment in not anticipating and justly estimating its inability to supply certain indispensable necessities." This is the main conclusion of Miss Lonn in her study of *Salt as a Factor in the Confederacy*, and it is a conclusion which may be applied to other items as well as salt. In controlling manufactures the government never aimed to do more than provide the army with essential supplies. Even the efforts in this direction were slow, halting, and indirect. The chief methods of influencing industrial production were the assignment or withholding of labor through manipulation of the draft, and the provision or denial of raw materials through control of the railroads.

Yet the government was "loath to enforce the kind of transportation policy the war effort demanded." At the start the railroad system of the South was, of course, defective. There were not enough railroad lines, and few of these were located where, strategically, they would do the most good. Besides, there were too many gaps, and there was too little rolling stock and too few mechanics and facilities for upkeep or repair. Despite these shortcomings, the railroads gave as much reality to the concept of "interior lines" as this concept ever attained. At the first battle of Bull Run the Confederates reinforced an army by railroad, in the midst of battle, for the first time in history. In moving General James Longstreet's men from Virginia to Tennessee before the battle of Chickamauga the Confederates again made history in the military use of railroads. Still, in the judgment of R. C. Black, historian of Confederate railroads, "the Confederates by no means made the best use of what they had." The government delayed too long in taking over and operating all the lines as a unified system. Confederate transportation often had to depend on wagons or carts, mule teams, and dirt roads. Instead of leaving teams and vehicles in the hands of owners, so as to let the economy go on functioning efficiently, the government too often impressed these things for strictly military uses. The resulting transportation difficulties, in the opinion of Charles W. Ramsdell, ranked next to fiscal policies in their "deleterious consequences" for the Confederacy. Without adequate transportation, the geographical advantages of the South were largely lost.

In their handling of finances, manufactures, and transportation, the Confederate leaders made a number of errors that have become clear enough in retrospect. So the question persists: Were the South's economic disasters to be blamed upon human failings rather than material inadequacies? Was Davis inferior to Lincoln, and Memminger to Salmon P. Chase, the Union treasury head, in economic statesmanship? Were Southern civilians inferior to Northern in business ability and capacity for work? It has been said that the Confederate civil leaders in general and Memminger in particular proved themselves incompetent. And yet, if we imagine Chase in Memminger's position, it is hard to believe that he could have made a reputation as a successful financier. Memminger had to deal with problems in comparison with which those of the Union treasury were almost child's play. As for the Southern people as a whole, they unquestionably lagged behind Northerners in business experience and in education and literacy, if not also in physical health. Yet it is hard to agree with the emphasis of Pollard when he concludes: "He who seeks to solve the problem of the downfall of the Southern Confederacy must take largely into consideration the absence of any intelligent and steady system in the conduct of public affairs; the little circles that bounded the Richmond administration; the deplorable want of the commercial or business facility in the Southern mind."

It is hard to believe, and impossible to prove, that the Southerners did a worse job with economic affairs than Northerners would have done in the same circumstances. It is unimportant and unnecessary to try to prove this. The point is that the North had an economic strength several times greater to start with. In order to overcome this handicap and attain even so much as equality in economic power, the civilians of the South would have had to be *several times* as able, man for man, as those of the North. And this, obviously, is too much to have expected of any people, however willing and determined they might have been.

If the South could not meet the North on anything like an equal economic footing, she would have to compensate in some other respect. She would have to be blessed with better luck or higher achievement in matters political, diplomatic, military, or psychological. A mere glance at these other considerations reveals at once that they cannot be appraised apart from one another, or the economic apart from any of them. These categories, after all, are purely arbitrary: we distinguish among them only for our own convenience.

In waging war, the Confederacy faced problems of politics and government that vastly complicated its problems of economic mobilization. Always the Southerners had to struggle with the incubus of John C. Calhoun, with the idea of state rights, with that fatal principle upon which their new government had been based. A Confederacy formed by particularist politicians could hardly be expected to adopt promptly those centralist policies—for marshaling resources and transportation—which victory demanded. Even apart from this ideological handicap, the Confederacy faced insuperable difficulties in attempting to set up, from scratch, a going administration in the midst of war. Professor Ramsdell has put the matter admirably: ". . . the southern people and their governments failed, with a few exceptions, to conserve, develop, and efficiently administer their resources; but it must be said that these were gigantic tasks, intricate, complex, and baffling. That they did not succeed better is not surprising when we remember the simplicity of southern economic and political organization before secession. There was not time, while a powerful and determined enemy was crashing at the gate, to reorganize their whole system and, without previous experience, create a complex administration, and train administrators. Problems had to be met as they arose. . . . All in all, it is not surprising that they could not be solved, or that, in the end, the collapse was complete."

By successful diplomacy, by winning the support of Great Britain or France, the South most likely could have canceled out all the economic advantages of the North. The Confederate financial policies, by the way, were not always easy to distinguish from the Confederate foreign policies. Thus, for example, the Erlanger loan, at least from the point of view of Judah P. Benjamin, was more a diplomatic than an economic measure, intended to elicit the support of France rather than, primarily, to raise funds. To explain why Southern hopes for foreign aid finally were dashed, it is necessary to look into a tangle of international economic relationships. It is necessary also to look into the world politics of the time, especially the divergent interests of Great Britain, France, and Russia. It is necessary even to look into the internal politics of England.

Certainly the economic history of the Confederacy cannot be told without including also the military and naval history (nor, for that matter, the military and naval without the economic). Bad as Southern transportation was at the start of the war, it soon was made worse by the advance of Union forces on land and sea. River and coastal waterways were occupied or blockaded and thus rendered useless to the Confederacy. Rail centers, like Chattanooga and Atlanta, were taken and new gaps thereby made in the already defective railroad system. The capture of New Orleans, only a year after the fighting had begun, meant the loss of the Confederacy's financial heart. As the Union armies took over more and more Southern territory, there was a continual shrinking of the area within which Confederate notes passed as money. And as this area contracted, the quantity of paper money in it increased even more rapidly than the treasury put forth new issues, for Southerners living in the occupied territory got rid of their Confederate money by sending it to places where it still had at least a little value—to places where the Stars and Bars still waved. The more ground the Confederacy lost in battle, the worse the problem of inflation became. Meanwhile, in filling her armies, the South had to draw off from the economy a much higher proportion of her manpower than the North did of hers. The South's capacity to produce, already so small by comparison, was made even smaller by a disproportionate reduction of her labor supply. While Union military power was weakening the Southern economy, Union naval power had the same effect in perhaps even greater degree. The blockade, by bringing about serious shortages in strategic items, not only added to the inflationary trends but also frustrated efforts to maintain the transportation network and to increase industrial output. And, toward the end of the war, the Southern loss of faith in victory, as has been seen, contributed to the currency depreciation and to the economic disorganization that ensued.

Thus psychological influences, resulting from military events, fatally affected economic conditions. The reverse is equally true. Economic conditions gave rise to psychological influences that seriously affected military events.

Strategy itself at times conformed to economic facts. When the South resorted to the draft, in April, 1862, the congressional critics of Davis blamed him for having made such an extreme measure necessary. They charged that he had adopted a strategy of the "dispersed defensive" and that this, in turn, had chilled the enthusiasm of Southern men, who would have volunteered in ample numbers for an aggressive, concentrated campaign against the North. In reply to his critics Davis explained that the Confederacy lacked the means for such a campaign. "Without military stores," he said, "without the workshops to create them, without the power to import them, necessity not choice has compelled us to occupy strong positions and everywhere to confront the enemy without reserves."

Soldier morale, presumably hurt by the dispersed defensive, was further damaged by economic developments behind the lines. As General Johnston remarks, "after the

Confederate currency had become almost worthless" the married soldiers from the farms "had to choose between their military service and the strongest obligations they knew—their duties to wives and children." The dilemma of these soldiers was made especially poignant by the actions of Confederate impressment officials. Those officials, as Johnston says, frequently preyed upon the most defenseless of the citizens, especially upon farm women whose husbands were away in the army. Hard beset by inflation and impressment, wives summoned their soldier-husbands home, and, faced with a torturing choice of loyalties, the soldiers often placed family above country. In other ways, too, the fiscal policies of the Confederacy no doubt impaired the morale of both soldiers and civilians. Amid the wild inflation some people grew rich overnight, at least on paper, and others lost their fortunes just as suddenly. A gambling spirit infected the land, and almost everybody became a speculator of some kind. Those gamblers who lost—and practically all of them lost in the end—naturally were prone to feelings of bitterness and envy. And they directed these feelings against one another as well as against the Yankee foe.

Since so much of the Southern despair was induced by objective conditions and events, on the battlefield and on the home front, it is difficult to accept the Wesley thesis that the Confederacy collapsed because of a failure of the spirit. In most respects the loss of morale seems to have been a secondary rather than a primary cause of defeat.

The prime cause must have been economic. Given the vast superiority of the North in men and materials, in instruments of production, in communication facilities, in business organization and skill—and assuming for the sake of the argument no more than rough equality in statecraft and generalship—the final outcome seems all but inevitable. At least, it seems to have become inevitable once two dangers for the Union had been passed. One of these was the threat of interference from abroad. The other was the possibility of military disaster resulting from the enemy's superior skill or luck on the battlefield, from his ability to make decisive use of his power-in-being before the stronger potential of the Union could be fully developed and brought into play. Both dangers appear to have been over by midsummer, 1863, if not already by autumn, 1862. Thereafter, month by month, the resources of the North began increasingly to tell, in what became more and more a war of attrition.

True, the victory is not always to the rich. The record of mankind offers many an example of a wealthy and fat and decadent people overcome by an enemy who was poor and lean and vigorous. Indeed, these historical examples heartened those Southerners who, at the outset, assumed that all Yankees had been corrupted by commerce and industry, that the "mudsills" of the factory and the money-grubbers of the counting-house would lack the fortitude that victory required. On the other hand, many in the North looked upon Southerners as a people debased, debauched, and incapacitated by contact with the institution of slavery. Today, at this distance in time, we can see that the two sides must have been about even in virtue and vice, devotion and disloyalty, human strength and weakness.

For the North to win, she had only to draw upon her resources as fully and as efficiently as the South drew upon hers; or, rather, the North had to make good use of only a fraction of her economic potential. Her material strength was so much greater that she could, as it were, almost lick the South with one hand tied behind her back. In fact, the North during the war years did devote a large part of her energies and resources to nonmilitary enterprise. Once the financial crisis of late 1861 was past, the Union entered upon an economic boom. She actually grew in material strength, while the South wasted away. From 1861 to 1865 nearly 5,000,000 acres of the public domain in the West were transferred to settlers and corporations. Railroad mileage lengthened from about 31,000 to more than 35,000 miles—an increase of approximately one-eighth. The value of imports for the North alone in 1864 was almost as great as it had been for the entire country, the South included, in 1860.

With justifiable pride President Abraham Lincoln boasted of the wartime progress and prosperity in his annual message to Congress of December, 1864. "It is of noteworthy interest," Lincoln declared, "that the steady expansion of population, improvement, and governmental institutions over the new and unoccupied portion of our country have scarcely been checked, much less impeded or destroyed, by our great civil war, which at first glance would seem to have absorbed almost the entire energies of the nation." He noted the sales of public land, the work on the Pacific railroad, the discovery and exploitation of gold and silver and mercury in the West. "The important fact remains demonstrated," he concluded, "that we have *more* men *now* than we had when the war *began*; that we are not exhausted, nor in process of exhaustion; that we are *gaining* strength, and may, if need be, maintain the contest indefinitely. This as to men. Material resources are now more complete and abundant than ever. The national resources . . . are unexhausted, and, as we believe, inexhaustible."

Jefferson Davis could not truthfully have said the same of the South in 1864. At that time the Confederacy was not yet beaten on the field of battle, but already economic exhaustion was setting in behind the lines. As Ramsdell has remarked, ". . . the Confederacy had begun to crumble, or to break down *within*, long before the military situation appeared to be desperate."

From Ramsdell's observation it is but a step to the conclusion that economic rather than strictly military superiority was the basic reason for the ultimate victory of the North. At the start the North had possessed no significant advantage in a narrowly military sense—certainly no advantage comparable to that of her economic power and potential. This vast productive ability made the Union armies the best fed, the best clothed, the best cared for that the world ever had seen. This economic might made it possible for the North to field the stronger forces and, when the final test came, to place at every crucial point, as A. B. Hart has said, "more officers, more men, more camp followers, and more army mules."

Some Northerners used to cherish a simple—and, it would seem, an irrefutable—explanation of the Northern victory. God had willed that the Union be preserved. Surely, in view of the disparity of resources, it would have taken a miracle, a direct intervention of the Lord on the other side, to enable the South to win. As usual, God was on the side of the heaviest battalions.

The Military Leadership of North and South

T. Harry Williams

GENERALS AND THEIR ART and their accomplishments have not been universally admired throughout the course of history. Indeed, there have been some who have sneered at even the successful captains of their time. Four centuries before Christ, Sophocles, as aware of the tragedy of war as he was of the tragedy of life, observed: "It is the merit of a general to impart good news, and to conceal the bad." And the Duke of Wellington, who knew from experience whereof he spoke, depreciated victory with the bitter opinion: "Nothing except a battle lost can be half so melancholy as a battle won."

Civil War generals were, of course, not considered sacrosanct—were, in fact, regarded as legitimate targets of criticism for anyone who had a gibe to fling. Senator Louis T. Wigfall was exercising his not inconsiderable talent for savage humor, usually reserved for the Davis administration, on the military when he said of John B. Hood: "That young man had a fine career before him until Davis undertook to make of him what the good Lord had not done—to make a great general of him." One can understand Assistant Secretary of War P. H. Watson's irritation when the War Department could not locate so important an officer as Joe Hooker on the eve of Second Manassas, while also noting Watson's patronizing attitude toward all generals in a letter to transportation director Herman Haupt stating that an intensive search for Hooker was being conducted in Willard's bar. "Be patient as possible with the Generals," Watson added. "Some of them will trouble you more than they will the enemy."

And yet in the final analysis, as those who have fought or studied war know, it is the general who is the decisive factor in battle. (At least, this has been true up to our own time, when war has become so big and dispersed that it may be said it is managed rather than commanded.) Napoleon put it well when he said, perhaps with some exaggeration: "The personality of the general is indispensable, he is the head, he is the all of an army. The Gauls were not conquered by the Roman legions, but by Caesar. It was not before the Carthaginian soldiers that Rome was made to tremble, but before Hannibal. It was not the Macedonian phalanx which penetrated to India, but Alexander. It was not the French Army which reached the Weser and the Inn, it was Turenne. Prussia was not defended for seven years against the three most formidable European Powers by the Prussian soldiers, but by Frederick the Great." This quotation may serve to remind us of another truth about war and generals that is often forgotten: That is that tactics is often a more decisive factor than strategy. The commander who has suffered a strategic reverse, Cyril Falls emphasizes, may remedy everything by a tactical success, whereas for a tactical reverse there may be no remedy whatever. Falls adds: "It is remarkable how many people exert themselves and go through contortions to prove that battles and wars are won by any means except that by which they are most commonly won, which is by fighting."

If, then, the general is so important in war, we are justified in asking, what are the qualities that make a general great or even just good? We may with reason look for clues to the answer in the writings of some of the great captains. But first of all, it may be helpful to list some qualities that, although they may be highly meritorious and desirable, are not sufficient in themselves to produce greatness. Experience alone is not enough. "A mule," said Frederick the Great, "may have made twenty campaigns under Prince Eugene and not be a better tactician for all that." Nor are education and intelligence the touchstones to measure a great general. Marshal Saxe went so far as to say: "Unless a man is born with a talent for war, he will never be other than a mediocre general." And Auguste Marmont, while noting that all the great soldiers had possessed "the highest faculties of mind," emphasized that they also had had something that was more important, namely, character.

What these last two commentators were trying to say was that a commander has to have in his make-up a mental strength and a moral power that enables him to dominate whatever event or crisis may emerge on the field of battle. Napoleon stated the case explicitly: "The first quality of a General-in-Chief is to have a cool head which receives exact impressions of things, which never gets heated, which never allows itself to be dazzled, or intoxicated, by good or bad news." Anyone who knows the Civil War can easily tick off a number of generals who fit exactly the pattern described next by Napoleon: "There are certain men who, on account of their moral and physical constitution, paint mental pictures out of everything: however exalted be their reason, their will, their courage, and whatever good qualities they may possess, nature has not fitted them to command armies, nor to direct great operations of war." Karl von Clausewitz said the same thing in a slightly different context. There are decisive moments in war, the German pointed out, when things no longer move of themselves, when "the machine itself"— the general's own army—begins to offer resistance. To overcome this resistance the commander must have "a great force of will." The whole inertia of the war comes to rest on his will, and only the spark of his own purpose and spirit can throw it off. This natural quality of toughness of fiber is especially important in measuring Civil War generalship because the rival generals were products of the same educational system and the same military background. As far as technique was concerned, they started equal, and differed only in matters of mind and character. It has been well said: "To achieve a Cannae a Hannibal is needed on the one side and a Terentius Varro on the other." And one may add, to achieve a Second Manassas a Robert E. Lee is needed on the one side and a John Pope on the other.

When Marshal Saxe enumerated the attributes of a

general, he named the usual qualities of intelligence and
courage, and then added another not always considered in
military evaluations—health. It is a factor that deserves
more attention than it has received. Clifford Dowdey has
recently reminded us of the effects of physical and mental
illness on the actions of the Confederate command at
Gettysburg. A comparison of the age levels of leading
Southern and Northern officers in 1861 is instructive. Although there are no significant differences in the ages of
the men who rose to division and corps generals, we note
that, of the officers who came to command armies for the
South, Albert Sidney Johnston was fifty-eight, Joseph E.
Johnston and Lee were fifty-four, John C. Pemberton was
forty-seven, Braxton Bragg was forty-four, and P. G. T.
Beauregard was forty-three. Of the Union army commanders, Hooker was forty-seven, Henry W. Halleck and
George G. Meade were forty-six, George H. Thomas was
forty-five, D. C. Buell was forty-three, William S. Rosecrans was forty-two, William T. Sherman was forty-one,
U. S. Grant was thirty-nine, Ambrose Burnside was thirty-
seven, and George B. McClellan was thirty-four. Hood
and Philip H. Sheridan at thirty represent the lowest age
brackets. Youth was clearly on the side of the Union, but
obviously it cannot be said, with any accuracy or finality,
that the generals in one particular age group did any better
than those in another. Nevertheless, when Grant thought
about the war in the years after, he inclined to place a
high premium on the qualities of youth, health, and energy, and doubted that a general over fifty should be
given field command. He recalled that during the war he
had had "the power to endure" anything. In this connection, it may be worthy of mention that during the Virginia
campaign of 1864 Lee was sick eleven of forty-four days,
while Grant was not indisposed for one.

The Civil War was pre-eminently a West Pointers' fight.
Of the sixty biggest battles, West Point graduates commanded both armies in fifty-five, and in the remaining five
a West Pointer commanded one of the opposing armies.

What were the men who would direct the blue and gray armies like in 1861? How well trained were they for war? What intellectual influences had formed their concepts of war and battle? A glance at the Point curriculum reveals that it was heavy on the side of engineering, tactics, and administration. The products of the academy came out with a good grounding in what may be termed the routine of military science. They knew how to train and administer a force of troops; or, to put it more accurately and to apply it specifically to the Civil War, they had the technical knowledge that enabled them to take over the administration of a large force without imposing too much strain on them or their men. It should be emphasized, however, that none of the West Pointers had had before 1861 any actual experience in directing troops in numbers. Not a one had controlled as large a unit as a brigade, and only a few had handled a regiment. Except for a handful of officers who had visited Europe, the men who would lead the Civil War hosts had never seen an army larger than the fourteen thousand men of Winfield Scott or Zachary Taylor in the Mexican War.

One subject which was taught but not emphasized at West Point was strategy, or the study of the higher art of war. The comparative subordination of strategy may be explained by the youth of the cadets and the feeling of the school's directors that it was more important to impart a basic knowledge of tactics and techniques to the boys. Nevertheless, many of the graduates enlarged their knowledge of the topic by reading books on military history while stationed at army posts. The strategy that was presented at the Point and studied by interested graduates came from a common source and had a common pattern. It was the product of the brilliant Swiss officer who had served with Napoleon, Antoine Henri Jomini, universally regarded as the foremost writer on the theory of war in the first half of the nineteenth century. Every West Point general in the war had been exposed to Jomini's ideas, either directly, by reading Jomini's writings or abridgments or expositions of them; or indirectly, by hearing them in the classroom or perusing the works of Jomini's American disciples. The influence of Jomini on the Civil War was profound, and this influence must be taken into account in any evaluation of Civil War generalship. There is little exaggeration in General J. D. Hittle's statement that "many a Civil War general went into battle with a sword in one hand and Jomini's *Summary of the Art of War* in the other."

Here it is impossible to attempt more than a summary of Jomini's ideas and writings. Essentially his purpose was to introduce rationality and system into the study of war. He believed that in war rules prevailed as much as in other areas of human activity and that generals should follow these rules. He sought to formulate a set of basic principles of strategy for commanders, using as his principal examples the campaigns and techniques of Napoleon. The most convenient approach to Jomini is through the four strategic principles that he emphasized, the famous principles that many Civil War generals could recite from memory:

(1) The commander should endeavor by strategic measures to bring the major part of his forces successively to bear on the decisive areas of the theater of war, while menacing the enemy's communications without endangering his own.

(2) He should maneuver in such a way as to engage the masses of his forces against fractions of the enemy.

(3) He should endeavor by tactical measures to bring his masses to bear on the decisive area of the battlefield or on the part of the enemy's line it was important to overwhelm.

(4) He should not only bring his masses to bear on the decisive point of the field but should put them in battle speedily and together in a simultaneous effort.

It is, perhaps, unnecessary to remark that much of this was not new. Xenophon had said about the same thing to the Greeks, and the definition of strategy as the art of bringing most of the strength of an army to bear on the decisive point has been fairly constant in the history of war. But it should be noted that Jomini envisioned the decisive point as the point where the enemy was weakest. This is often true but not always. There are occasions in war when the decisive point may be the strongest one, as Epaminondas demonstrated at Leuctra and the American strategists in the cross-Channel attack of World War II.

To explain how his principles should be applied in war, Jomini worked out an elaborate doctrine based on geometrical formations. He loved diagrams, and devised twelve model plans of battle; some Civil War generals actually tried to reproduce on the field some of these neat paper exercises. In all Jomini's plans there was a theater of operations, a base of operations, a zone of operations, and so forth. The smart commander chose a line of operations that would enable him to dominate three sides of the rectangular zone; this accomplished, the enemy would have to retire or face certain defeat. Jomini talked much of concentric and eccentric maneuver and interior and exterior lines, being the first theorist to emphasize the advantage of the former over the latter.

At times, especially when he discussed the advantage of the offensive—and he always stressed the offensive—Jomini seemed to come close to Clausewitz's strategy of annihilation. But a closer perusal of his writings reveals that he and the German were far apart. Although Jomini spoke admiringly of the hard blow followed by the energetic pursuit, his line of operation strategy allowed the enemy the option of retiring. In reality Jomini thought that the primary objectives in war were places rather than armies: the occupation of territory or the seizure of such "decisive strategic points" as capitals. He affected to be the advocate of the new Napoleonic ways of war, but actually he looked back instead of forward. It has been rightly said of him (in R. A. Preston, S. F. Wise, and H. O. Werner, *Men in Arms*): "By his emphasis on lines of operation Jomini, in effect, returned to the eighteenth-century method of approaching the study of war as a geometric exercise. . . . In emphasizing the continuance of traditional features he missed the things that were new.

There can be no doubt that this interpreter of Napoleonic warfare actually set military thought back into the eighteenth century, an approach which the professional soldiers of the early nineteenth century found comfortable and safe."

Jomini confessed that he disliked the destructiveness of the warfare of his time. "I acknowledge," he wrote, "that my prejudices are in favor of the good old times when the French and English guards courteously invited each other to fire first as at Fontenoy. . . ." He said that he preferred "chivalric war" to "organized assassination," and he deplored as particularly cruel and terrible what he called wars of "opinion," or as we would say today, of "ideas." War was, as it should be, most proper and polite when it was directed by professional soldiers and fought by professional armies for limited objectives. All this is, of course, readily recognizable as good eighteenth-century doctrine. This could be Marshal Saxe saying: "I do not favor pitched battles . . . and I am convinced that a skillful general could make war all his life without being forced into one." Eighteenth-century warfare was leisurely and its ends were limited. It stressed maneuver rather than battle, as was natural in an age when professional armies were so expensive to raise and maintain that they could not be risked unless victory was reasonably certain. It was conducted with a measure of humanity that caused Chesterfield to say: "War is pusillanimously carried on in this degenerate age; quarter is given; towns are taken and people spared; even in a storm, a woman can hardly hope for the benefit of a rape." Most important of all, war was regarded as a kind of exercise or game to be conducted by soldiers. For the kings war might have a dynastic objective, but in the thinking of many military men it had little if any relationship to society or politics or statecraft.

Many West Pointers—McClellan, Lee, Sherman, and Beauregard, among others—expressed their admiration of Jomini and usually in extravagent terms. Halleck devoted years to translating Jomini's works, and his own book on the elements of war was only a rehash of Jomini, in parts, in fact, a direct steal. William Hardee's manual on tactics reflected Jominian ideas. But the American who did more than any other to popularize Jomini was Dennis Hart Mahan, who began teaching at West Point in 1824 and who influenced a whole generation of soldiers. He interpreted Jomini both in the classroom and in his writings. At one time Jomini's own works had been used at the academy but had been dropped in favor of abridgments by other writers. In 1848 Mahan's book on war, usually known by the short title of *Outpost*, became an official text. Most of the Civil War generals had been Mahan's pupils, and those older ones who had not, like Lee, were exposed to his ideas through personal relationships or through his book. Probably no one man had a more direct and formative impact on the thinking of the war's commanders.

Mahan, of course, did little more than to reproduce Jomini's ideas. He talked much of the principle of mass, of defeating the enemy's fractions in succession, and of interior lines. But it should be emphasized that his big point, the one he dwelt on most, was the offensive executed by celerity of movement. Mahan never tired of stressing the advantage of rapidity in war—or of excoriating "the slow and over-prudent general" who was afraid to grasp victory. "By rapidity of movement we can . . . make war feed war," he wrote. "We disembarrass ourselves of those immense trains." There was one operation that could change the face of a war, he said. When one's territory was invaded, the commander should invade the territory of the enemy; this was the mark of "true genius." (This passage makes us think immediately of Lee and Stonewall Jackson.) Jominian strategy as interpreted by Mahan then was the mass offensive waged on the battlefield, perhaps with utmost violence, but only on the battlefield. It cannot be sufficiently emphasized that Mahan, like his master, made no connection between war and technology and national life and political objectives. War was still an exercise carried on by professionals. War and statecraft were still separate things.

The Jominian influence on Civil War military leadership was obviously profound and pervasive. But before considering its manifestations, it may be helpful to dispose of a number of generals who do not meet the criteria of greatness or even of acceptable competence. This perhaps too brutal disposal will be performed by means of some undoubtedly too sweeping generalizations. These generals fell short of the mark partly because, as will be developed later, they were too thorough Jominians, and partly because they lacked the qualities of mind and character found in the great captains of war. Of the generals who commanded armies we can say that the following had such grave shortcomings that either they were not qualified to command or that they can be classified as no better than average soldiers: on the Union side—McClellan, Burnside, Hooker, Meade, Buell, Halleck, and Rosecrans; on the Confederate side—Albert Sidney Johnston, Beauregard, Bragg, Joe Johnston, and Edmund Kirby Smith.

McClellan will be discussed later, but here we may anticipate by saying that he did not have the temperament required for command. Burnside did not have the mentality. Hooker was a fair strategist, but he lacked iron and also the imagination to control troops not within his physical vision. Meade was a good routine soldier but no more, and was afflicted with a defensive psychosis. Buell was a duplicate of McClellan without any color. Halleck was an unoriginal scholar and an excellent staff officer who should never have taken the field. Rosecrans had strategic ability but no poise or balance; his crack-up at Chickamauga is a perfect example of Napoleon's general who paints the wrong kind of mental picture. A. S. Johnston died before he could prove himself, but nothing that he did before his death makes us think that he was anything but a gallant troop leader. Beauregard probably was developing into a competent commander by the time of Shiloh, but his failure to win that battle plus his personality faults caused him to be exiled to comparatively minor posts for the rest of the war. Bragg, the general of the lost opportunity, was a good deal like Hooker. He created favorable situations but lacked the determination to carry through his purpose; he did not have the will to overcome the inertia of war. Kirby Smith made a promising start but seemed to shrink under the responsibility of command and finally disappeared into the backwash of the Trans-Mississippi theater. The stature of Joe Johnston probably will be argued as long as there are Civil War fans to talk. But surely we can take his measure by his decision in the Georgia campaign to withdraw from a position near Cassville that he termed the "best that I saw occupied during the war" merely because his corps generals advised retiring. A great general, we feel, would have delivered the attack that Johnston originally planned to make. Johnston undoubtedly had real ability, but he never did much with it. It is reasonable to expect that a general who has sustained opportunities will sometime, once, achieve something decisive. Certainly Johnston had the opportunities, but there is no decisive success on his record.

Of the lesser generals, it is fair to say that James Longstreet and Stonewall Jackson were outstanding corps leaders, probably the best in the war, but that neither gave much evidence of being able to go higher. Longstreet failed in independent command. Jackson performed brilliantly as commander of a small army but probably lacked the administrative ability to handle a large one. In addition, he was never fairly tested against first-rate opposition. Thomas and W. S. Hancock stand out among Union corps generals. Thomas also commanded an army, but his skills were of a particular order and could be exercised only in a particular situation. He excelled in the counterattack delivered from strength. J. E. B. Stuart, Sheridan, N. B. Forrest, and J. H. Wilson were fine cavalry leaders, but we cannot say with surety that they could have been anything else. On the one occasion when Sheridan directed an army he displayed unusual ability to handle combined arms (infantry, cavalry, artillery), but he enjoyed such a preponderant advantage in numbers over his opponent as to be almost decisive. He was never really subjected to the inertia of war. In the last analysis, the only Civil

War generals who deserve to be ranked as great are Lee for the South and Grant and Sherman for the North.

We can now turn to an examination of the influence of Jominian eighteenth-century military thought on Civil War generalship, first directing our attention to the first Northern generals with whom Abraham Lincoln had to deal. It is immediately and painfully evident that in the first of the world's modern wars these men were ruled by traditional concepts of warfare. The Civil War was a war of ideas and, inasmuch as neither side could compromise its political purposes, it was a war of unlimited objectives. Such a war was bound to be a rough, no-holds-barred affair, a bloody and brutal struggle. Yet Lincoln's generals proposed to conduct it in accordance with the standards and the strategy of an earlier and easier military age. They saw cities and territory as their objectives rather than the armies of the enemy. They hoped to accomplish their objectives by maneuvering rather than by fighting. McClellan boasted that the "brightest chaplets" in his history were Manassas and Yorktown, both occupied after the Confederates had departed, because he had seized them by "pure military skill" and without the loss of life. When he had to lose lives, McClellan was almost undone. The "sickening sight" of the battlefield, he told his wife after Fair Oaks, took all the charms from victory. McClellan's mooning around the field anguishing over the dead may seem strange to the modern mind, but Jomini would have understood his reactions. Buell argued, in the spirit of Marshal Saxe, that campaigns could be carried out and won without engaging in a single big battle. Only when success was reasonably certain should a general risk battle, Buell said, adding: "War has a higher object than that of mere bloodshed." After the Confederates retired from Corinth, Halleck instructed his subordinates: "There is no object in bringing on a battle if this object can be obtained without one. I think by showing a bold front for a day or two the enemy will continue his retreat, which is all I desire." Meade, who confessed shame for his cause when he was ordered to seize the property of a Confederate sympathizer, thought that the North should prosecute the war "like the afflicted parent who is compelled to chastise his erring child, and who performs the duty with a sad heart."

With an almost arrogant assurance, Lincoln's first generals believed that war was a business to be carried on by professionals without interference from civilians and without political objectives. It is no exaggeration to say that some of the officers saw the war as a kind of game played by experts off in some private sphere that had no connection with the government or society. Rosecrans gave a typical expression of this viewpoint when he resisted pressure from Washington to advance before the battle of Stone's River: "I will not move until I am ready! . . . War is a business to be conducted systematically. I believe I understand my business. . . . I will not budge until I am ready." But, as might be expected, the classic example is McClellan. He refused to retain General Charles Hamilton in his army when Lincoln requested him to, even after, or more accurately, especially after the President emphasized that there were weighty political reasons for assigning Hamilton a minor position. When McClellan conceived his Urbanna plan, he did not tell Lincoln about it for months. He did not seem to know that it was his job to counsel his political superior on his plans; in fact, he did not seem to know that there was any relationship between war and politics. In the winter of 1861–1862 Lincoln implored McClellan to make a move, even a small or diversionary one, to inspire public opinion with the belief that more decisive action was contemplated later. McClellan refused on the grounds that he was not yet completely prepared. That the public might become so discouraged that it would abandon the war impressed McClellan not at all. With him the only question was when the professionals would be ready to start the game.

Lincoln's early generals also accepted blindly the Jominian doctrine of concentration. As they interpreted it, it meant one big effort at a time in one theater. McClellan's proposal to mass 273,000 troops in the eastern department in 1861, a physical and military impossibility at that time, was a typical piece of Jominian thinking. Of course, each commander was convinced that the one big push should be made by him, and each one demanded that other departments be stripped of troops to strengthen his own army. It would be possible to argue that the apparent caution of every Union general in the first years of the war, and the consequent inaction of Union armies, was the result of each commander's conviction that he did not possess enough strength to undertake the movements recommended by Jomini. But this feeling of the generals brought them into conflict with their commander in chief, who was no Jominian in his strategic notions, and their differences with Lincoln will be discussed later.

When we examine the psychology of the Northern generals, the thought immediately occurs that the Southern generals were not like this, and inevitably we ask, why not? Had the Southerners freed themselves from Jomini's dogma? Were they developing new ways of war? The answer to both questions is no. The Confederates were, if possible, more Jominian than the Federals. They simply gave a different emphasis to the traditional pattern of strategic thought. Whereas the Federals borrowed from Jomini the idea of places as objectives, the Confederates took from him the principle of the offensive. Moreover, the Southern generals were fortunate in being able to make enemy armies the object of their offensives because Confederate policy did not look to the acquisition of enemy territory. The influence of Mahan, with his doctrine of celerity and the headlong attack, is also apparent in Confederate strategy, especially as it was employed by Lee. In addition, the poverty of Southern resources had the effect of forcing Southern generals to think in aggressive terms. They could not afford to wait for a big build-up in men and equipment, but had to act when they could with what they had. Paradoxically, the Industrial Revolution, which would have so much to do with bringing about the advent of total war with all its destructiveness, had the immediate consequence of making the Northern generals less inclined to deal out destruction. They could secure material so easily that they refused to move until they had received more than they needed—after which they were often so heavily laden they could not move.

Far from departing from Jomini, the Confederates were the most brilliant practitioners of his doctrine. If we look for successful applications of the principles that Jomini emphasized—the objective, the offensive, mass, economy of force, interior lines, and unity of command—we find them most frequently in the Confederate campaigns and most particularly in the Virginia theater. Lee, the Confederacy's best general, was also its greatest Jominian. Probably it is because Lee embodied so precisely the spirit of traditional warfare that he has been ranked so high by students of war. Military historians are likely to be as conservative as generals. The English writers, who have done so much to form our image of the war, have been especially lavish in their praise. It may be suspected that their attitude stems largely from a feeling that Lee was a gentleman, English style, although for a long while the British, when they faced a possible combination of superior continental powers, studied Lee's strategy because of its application of the principle of interior lines. Cyril Falls said that Lee was a master combination of "strategist, tactical genius, leader of the highest inspiration, and technician in the arts of hastily fortifying defensive positions superbly chosen." Falls added: "He must stand as the supreme figure of this survey of a hundred years of war." Colonel A. H. Burne was more restrained, but spoke admiringly of Lee's audacity, his use of the offensive, and his skill at concentration. The opinions of G. F. R. Henderson and G. J. Wolseley are so well known as not to require quotation.

Let us concede that many of the tributes to Lee are deserved. He was not all that his admirers have said of him, but he was a large part of it. But let us also note that even his most fervent admirers, when they come to evaluate him as a strategist, have to admit that his abilities were never demonstrated on a larger scale than a theater. Cyril Falls, after his extravagant eulogy of Lee, falls on his face in attempting to attribute to his subject gifts for "large-scale strategy": the only example he can find is Lee's redeployment of forces between the Shenandoah Valley and Richmond during the Peninsula campaign! Lee was preeminently a field or a theater strategist, and a great one, but it remains unproven that he was anything more or wanted to be anything more. "In spite of all his ability, his heroism and the heroic efforts of his army," writes General J. F. C. Fuller, "because he would think and work in a corner, taking no notice of the whole, taking no interest in forming policy or in the economic side of the war, he was ultimately cornered and his cause lost." For his preoccupation with the war in Virginia, Lee is not to be criticized. He was a product of his culture, and that culture, permeated in its every part by the spirit of localism, dictated that his outlook on war should be local. Nevertheless, it must be recognized that his restricted view constituted a tragic command limitation in a modern war. The same limitation applied to Southern generalship as a whole. The Confederates, brilliant and bold in executing Jominian strategy on the battlefield, never succeeded in lifting their gifts above the theater level.

In many respects Lee was not a modern-minded general. He probably did not understand the real function of a staff and certainly failed to put together an adequate staff for his army. Although he had an excellent eye for terrain, his use of maps was almost primitive. He does not seem to have appreciated the impact of railroads on warfare or to have realized that railroads made Jomini's principle of interior lines largely obsolete. His mastery of logistics did not extend beyond departmental limits. In February, 1865, he said that he could not believe Sherman would be able to move into North Carolina. The evidence of Sherman's great march was before him, and yet he was not quite sure it had really happened.

The most striking lack of modernity in Lee was his failure to grasp the vital relationship between war and statecraft. Here the great Virginian was truly a Jominian. Almost as much as McClellan, he thought of war as a professional exercise. One of his officers said admiringly that Lee was too thorough a soldier to attempt to advise the government on such matters as the defense of Richmond. When late in the war a cabinet member asked Lee for his opinion on the advisability of moving the capital farther south, the general replied: "That is a political question . . . and you politicians must determine it. I shall endeavor to take care of the army, and you must make the laws and control the Government." And yet what could be a more strategic question than the safety of the capital? Lee attained a position in the Confederacy held by no other man, either in civil or military life. There was little exaggeration in the statement General William Mahone made to him: "You are the State." But Lee could not accept the role that his eminence demanded. He could never have said as Pitt did: "I know that I can save the country and that no one else can." It has been suggested that Lee did not try to impose his will on the government because of his humility of character, and this may well be true. But it would also seem to be true that he did not know that a commander had any political responsibility.

Lincoln's first generals did not understand that war and statecraft were parts of the same piece. But none of the Confederate generals, first or last, ever grasped this fact about modern war. The most distinguishing feature of Southern generalship is that it did not grow. Lee and the other Confederate commanders were pretty much the same men in 1865 that they had been in 1861. They were good, within certain limits, at the beginning, and they were good at the end but still within the original limits. They never freed themselves from the influence of traditional doctrine. The probable explanation, David Donald has suggested, is that the Confederates won their first battles with Jominian strategy and saw no reason to change and that the Southern mind, civil and military, was unreceptive to new ideas. The North, on the other hand, finally brought forward generals who were able to grow and who could employ new ways of war. Even so doctrinaire a Jominian as Halleck reached the point where he could approve techniques of total war that would have horrified the master. But the most outstanding examples of growth and originality among the Northern generals are Grant and Sherman.

The qualities of Grant's generalship deserve more analysis than those of Lee, partly because they have not been sufficiently emphasized but largely because Grant was a more modern soldier than his rival. First, we note that Grant had that quality of character or will exhibited by all the great captains. (Lee had it, too.) Perhaps the first military writer to emphasize this trait in Grant was C. F. Atkinson in 1908. Grant's distinguishing feature as a general, said Atkinson, was his character, which was controlled by a tremendous will; with Grant action was translated from thought to deed by all the force of a tremendous personality. This moral strength of Grant's may be news to some present-day historians, but it was overpoweringly apparent to all who were thrown into close association with him. Charles Francis Adams, Jr., like all his family not disposed to easy praise, said that Grant was really an extraordinary person, although he did not look it. In a crisis, Adams added, all would instinctively lean on Grant. Lincoln saw this quality in Grant clearly: "The great thing about Grant, I take it, is his perfect coolness and persistency of purpose. I judge he is not easily excited, —which is a great element in an officer." But the best tribute to Grant's character was paid by the general who knew him best. In a typical explosive comment to J. H. Wilson, Sherman said: "Wilson, I am a damn sight smarter than Grant. I know a great deal more about war, military history, strategy, and administration, and about everything else than he does. But I tell you where he beats me, and where he beats the world. He don't care a damn for what the enemy does out of his sight, but it scares me like hell." On the eve of the great campaigns of 1864 Sherman wrote to Grant that he considered Grant's strongest feature was his ability to go into battle without hesitation, doubts, or reserve. Characteristically Sherman added "It was this that made me act with confidence."

In this same letter Sherman confessed to a reservation that he had had about Grant: "My only points of doubt were as to your knowledge of grand strategy, and of books of science and history; but I confess your common sense seems to have supplied all this." Common sense Grant had, and it enabled him to deal with such un-Jominian phenomena as army correspondents and political generals. Unlike Sherman, Grant accepted the reporters—but he rendered them harmless. "General Grant informs us correspondents that he will willingly facilitate us in obtaining all proper information," Junius Browne wrote S. H. Gay, then added significantly that Grant was "not very communicative." Unlike McClellan, who would not accept General Hamilton for political considerations urged by Lincoln, Grant took John A. McClernand at the President's request. He could not imagine why Lincoln wanted a command for McClernand but assumed that there must be some reason important to his civil superior. He put up with McClernand until he found a way to strike him down to which Lincoln could not object. In this whole affair Grant showed that he realized the vital relation between politics and modern war.

It was Grant's common sense that enabled him to rise above the dogmas of traditional warfare. On one occasion a young officer, thinking to flatter Grant, asked his opinion of Jomini. Grant replied that he had never read the master. He then expressed his own theory of strategy: "The art of war is simple enough. Find out where your enemy is. Get at him as soon as you can. Strike at him as hard as you can and as often as you can, and keep moving on." After the war Grant discussed more fully his opinion of the value of doctrine. He conceded that military knowledge was highly desirable in a commander. But he added: "If men make war in slavish observance of rules, they will fail. No rules will apply to conditions of war as different as those which exist in Europe and Amer-

ica. . . . War is progressive, because all the instruments
and elements of war are progressive." He then referred to
the movement that had been his most striking departure
from the rules, the Vicksburg campaign. To take Vicksburg by rules would have required a withdrawal to Memphis, the opening of a new line of operations, in fact, a
whole new strategic design. But Grant believed that the
discouraged condition of Northern opinion would not permit such a conformity to Jominian practice: "In a popular
war we had to consider political exigencies." It was this
ability of Grant's to grasp the political nature of modern
war that marks him as the first of the great modern
generals.

The question of where to rank Sherman among Civil
War generals has always troubled military writers. He is
obviously not a Jominian, and just as obviously he is not
a great battle captain like Grant or Lee. Colonel Burne
points out that never once did Sherman command in a
battle where he engaged his whole force and that he never
won a resounding victory. Conceding that in the Georgia
campaign Sherman displayed imagination, resource, ver-
satility, broadness of conception, and genuine powers of
leadership—all fundamental traits of a great commander
—Burne still contends that Sherman exhibited two serious
failings: that of pursuing a geographical rather than a
military objective and that of avoiding risk. B. H. Liddell
Hart, on the other hand, depicts Sherman as the greatest
general of the war because more than any other commander he came to see that the object of strategy is to
minimize fighting. Part of this evaluation can be written
off as an attempt by Liddell Hart to glorify through Sherman the British strategy of the "indirect approach." And
yet he is right in saying that Sherman had the most complete grasp of the truth that the resisting power of a
modern democracy depends heavily on the popular will
and that this will depends in turn on a secure economic and
social basis. Sherman, a typical Jominian at the beginning
of the war, became its greatest exponent of economic and
psychological warfare. Nobody realized more clearly than

Sherman the significance of the techniques he introduced. Describing to Grant what he meant to do on his destructive march, he said, "This may not be war, but rather statesmanship." At the same time we must recognize that Sherman's strategy by itself would not have brought the Confederacy down. That end called for a Grant who at the decisive moment would attack the enemy's armed forces. As Burne puts it: "Sherman might help to prepare the ground, but it was Grant who struck the blow." The North was fortunate in finding two generals who between them executed Clausewitz's three objectives of war: to conquer and destroy the enemy's armed forces, to get possession of the material elements of aggression and other sources of existence of the enemy, and to gain public opinion by winning victories that depress the enemy's morale.

It remains to touch on the military leadership of the North and the South at the highest levels where strategy was determined—at the rival Presidents and the command systems they headed. In supreme leadership the Union was clearly superior. Lincoln was an abler and a stronger man than Davis. The Northern President illustrated perfectly the truth of Clausewitz's dictum that "a remarkable, superior mind and strength of character" are the primary qualifications of a director of war. The North developed at an early date an over-all plan of strategy, and it finally devised a unified command system for the entire military machine. The South was unable to accomplish either one of these objectives. But its failure should not be set down as the result of a shortage of brains among its leaders. Here again we need to remind ourselves that ways of making war are always the product of cultures. For the nationalistic North it was comparatively easy to achieve a broad view of war. Conversely, it was natural for the localistic South to adopt a narrow view and to fight a conservative war. Confederate strategy was almost wholly defensive, and was designed to guard the whole circumference of the country. In military jargon, it was a cordon defense. Probably the South's best chance to win its independence by a military decision was to attempt on a grand strategic scale the movement its generals were so good at on specific battlefields—the concentrated mass offensive. But the restrictions of Southern culture prevented any national application of the one Jominian principle that might have brought success.

Just as a cordon defense was the worst strategy for the South, a cordon offense was the best strategy for the North. This was the strategy that Lincoln had pressed upon his generals almost from the beginning of the war —to make enemy armies their objective and to move all Federal forces against the enemy line simultaneously. An offensive along the entire circumference of the Confederacy would prevent the enemy from moving troops from one threatened point to another and would inevitably achieve a break-through. It was an eminently sensible strategy for the side with the greater numbers and the superior lines of transportation and for a war fought over such a vast theater. When Lincoln proposed his plan to general after general, it met with polite scorn. It violated the Jominian principle of concentration in one theater for one big effort. It was the product of a mind that did not know the rules of war.

Not until he found Grant did Lincoln find a general who was original enough to employ his strategy. Grant's master design for 1864 called for an advance of Federal armies all along the line. It was the operation that broke the back of the Confederacy. When Grant explained his plan to the President, he remarked that even the smaller Federal forces not fighting would help the fighting by advancing and engaging the attention of the enemy. We have dealt much with maxims here, and we may fittingly conclude with one. Lincoln grasped Grant's point immediately and uttered a maxim of his own. At least for the Civil War it had more validity than anything written by Baron Jomini. "Those not skinning can hold a leg," said the commander in chief.

Northern Diplomacy and European Neutrality

Norman A. Graebner

MAJOR ROBERT ANDERSON'S surrender of Fort Sumter in April, 1861, placed an unprecedented burden on American diplomacy. Not since the American Revolution had the foreign relations of the United States been reduced to a defense of the Republic's very existence. Diplomacy, to be sure, was only one element in the vast arsenal of resources upon which Northern leadership could draw to frustrate the South's determination to sever the Union, but from the outset of the struggle it assumed a primary importance. Even limited European power, thrown effectively into the scale against the North, could have rendered the Southern cause successful. The nation's future, therefore, rested on the efficiency of its diplomatic as much as its military corps.

Europe's involvement in the American Civil War comprised a persistent danger to the Union, for the Southern independence movement threatened all the fundamental power relationships between the Old World and the New. Despite its tradition of isolationism toward Europe, the American Republic had become by 1861 a significant force in world politics. Cassius Clay, President Lincoln's choice for the court at St. Petersburg, wrote in April, 1862, that it was "useless to deceive ourselves with the idea that we can isolate ourselves from European interventions. We became in spite of ourselves—the Monroe Doctrine—Washington's farewell—and all that—a part of the 'balance of power.'" To European leaders the United States was a nation of consequence in world affairs, but the relationship of American strength and American traditions to the precise interests of Europe varied from country to country.

London promised to become the focal point of all wartime diplomatic maneuvering, for Britain was the dominant power of Europe and her control of Canada and the sea lanes of the north Atlantic created extensive commitments in the New World. France was equally concerned over events in America but lacked the power to escape the British lead. Keeping such interested and calculating nations neutral became the chief task of Northern diplomacy.

Fortunately for the North, Anglo-American relations had never been more cordial than they were in 1861. But this was no guarantee of British neutrality. Britain's powerful conservative classes, always cynical toward the democratic experiment of the United States, recognized the fundamental meaning of the American Civil War. Democratic institutions were on trial. The United States as a nation had passed beyond the normal control of Old World power, but if the American people were determined to destroy their national greatness and demonstrate the failure of their institutions, the least that reactionary Europe could do was to encourage them in their effort so that the work of destruction might succeed. British aristocrats had long regarded the American democratic example as a threat to their estate. For them the breakup of the American Union would impede the expansion of democracy everywhere. In July, 1861, *Blackwood's Magazine* declared: "It is precisely because we do *not* share the admiration of America for her own institutions and political tendencies that we do not now see in the impending change an event altogether to be deplored."

British conservatives resented American power and truculence as much as American institutions. What disturbed them especially was the growth of the United States into a formidable maritime rival. Edouard de Stoeckl, the Russian Minister in Washington, lamented in January, 1860, that in the approaching dissolution of the Union Great Britain would experience one of those "strokes of fortune" which occur but rarely in history. England, he predicted, would benefit more than any other nation from the disintegration of American power. "The Cabinet of London," he warned his government, "is watching attentively the internal dissensions of the Union and awaits the result with an impatience which it has difficulty in disguising." From St. Petersburg Cassius Clay warned Lincoln, "I saw at a glance where the feeling of England was. They hoped for our ruin! They are jealous of our power. They care neither for the South nor the North. They hate both."

Western Europe, moreover, had long been indignant at the American effort to keep the Western Hemisphere off limits for further European encroachment. For the ambitious Louis Napoleon of France, especially, events in America were encouraging, for they seemed to be rendering the Monroe Doctrine inoperative. No American fleet would block the contemplated movement of French troops to Vera Cruz or demolish his dreams of establishing a vassal empire in Mexico. A strong and friendly Confederate States of America would create a buffer between what remained of the United States and his new Mexican possessions. Secession appeared so consequential to Europe because it again exposed the western world to European partition. It was no wonder that Stoeckl advised his government in April, 1861, that "England will take advantage of the first opportunity to recognize the seceded States and that France will follow her."

In Washington, Henri Mercier, the French Minister, favored immediate action. He advised his government that in recognizing the Confederacy it would give the American conflict the character of a war and thereby extend to French seamen the benefit of neutral rights. The United States could not complain, he added, because it had recognized the revolutionary governments of Spanish America. Certainly this nation could not be offended merely because other nations accepted its democratic principles of self-determination. Yet Mercier was a realist. He admonished the French Minister in Paris to formulate his American policy only in agreement with the other powers of Europe.

Russia alone of the European states made the preservation of the Union a matter of conscious policy. For Stoeckl the destruction of the Union threatened the equilibrium of world politics. The United States, ran his argument, had become Europe's best guarantee against British aggression and arrogance. Traditional Russian-American friendship had been based on a mutual rivalry toward Great Britain. It had been the case of the enemies of a rival becoming friends. George Mifflin Dallas, when United States Minister at the Czar's court during the Van Buren administration, had recorded this significant phrase of Nicholas I, "Not only are our interests alike, our enemies are the same." [1]

After the outbreak of the Civil War the *Journal of St. Petersburg*, official organ of the Czarist government, declared: "Russia entertains for the United States of America a lively sympathy founded on sentiments of mutual friendship and on common interests. She considers their prosperity necessary to the general equilibrium." Nothing, the Imperial Cabinet agreed, should be permitted to weaken this powerful counterpoise to England. Prince Gortchakov, the Russian Foreign Minister, instructed Stoeckl in July, 1861, to assure the American nation that it could assume "the most cordial sympathy on the part of our August Master, during the serious crisis which it is passing through at present." This *entente cordiale* between the world's greatest despotism and its leading democracy was *Realpolitik* at its diplomatic best, for despite the incompatibility of political principles, it served the best interests of both nations.

William H. Seward, Lincoln's Secretary of State, assumed the essential task of preventing the introduction of European power into the American Civil War. His diplomacy had but one objective—the preservation of the Union. Seward's devotion to this cause was so intense that in April, 1861, he recommended to Lincoln a foreign war, perhaps against Spain and France, to rally the seceded states around the American flag and thus reforge the Union. Lincoln tactfully ignored the proposal, but the Washington diplomatic corps was amazed. Lord Lyons, the British Minister, warned the Foreign Office in London that Seward would be "a dangerous foreign minister."

Thereafter the British government regarded the American Secretary with suspicion. Charles Francis Adams, the American Minister in London, reported that Seward was viewed there as "an ogre fully resolved to eat all Englishmen raw." Lord John Russell, the British Foreign Secretary, addressed Lyons in February, 1861: "The success or failure of Mr. Seward's plans to prevent the disruption of the North American Union is a matter of deep interest to Her Majesty's Government." From the opening guns of the war Seward's leadership was a matter of grave concern to the chancelleries of Europe.

To forestall European interference in American affairs after the fall of Sumter, Seward denied officially the existence of any war between North and South. "There is here, as there always has been," he informed the British and French governments, "one political power, namely, the United States of America, competent to make war and peace, and conduct commerce and alliances with all foreign nations." What existed, he explained, was an armed sedition seeking to overthrow the government. Its suppression did not constitute a war or in any manner modify the character, rights, and responsibilities of either the United States or foreign nations in their diplomatic relationships. Seward admitted that international law permitted the recognition of established *de facto* governments; he merely denied that one existed in the South.

What endangered Seward's rigid position toward Europe was the rapid expansion of the conflict between North and South onto the Atlantic. It was fundamental in Lincoln's strategy to weaken and destroy the Southern economy by cutting off Southern shipments of cotton to Europe through a blockade of the Southern ports. Shortly after the crisis of Fort Sumter the Confederate government issued a proclamation calling for privateers, and Lincoln announced his blockade. Seward warned Lyons that the North would tolerate no further European commerce with the South, but he denied that a formal blockade destroyed his own claims that war did not exist. Yet the United States could hardly proclaim a blockade without declaring itself a belligerent and claiming rights over foreign vessels admitted only in time of war. Lyons was disturbed, for the blockade imposed on Europe the choice of recognizing the Confederacy or submitting to the interruption of its commerce with the South.

Britain, fearful of being trapped in a maritime war, took immediate steps to protect her commerce. On May 13, 1861, without awaiting the arrival of Minister Adams, Queen Victoria issued a declaration of neutrality which called upon British subjects to avoid hostilities between the North and South. Soon France, Spain, the Netherlands, and Brazil followed the British lead. This recognition of Southern belligerency granted to Southern ships the privileges in neutral ports accorded the ships of the Federal government.

Washington was shocked at this British action, for it not only suggested collusion between Britain and France but also presaged the diplomatic recognition of the South. Charles Sumner, the Massachusetts Senator, termed the Queen's proclamation "the most hateful act of English history since the time of Charles 2nd." Seward's reaction was even more violent. "They have misunderstood things fearfully, in Europe," he wrote home in May. "Great Britain is in great danger of sympathizing so much with the South for the sake of peace and cotton as to drive us to make war against her, as the ally of the traitors. . . . It will be dreadful but the end will be sure and swift." Through Adams in London, Seward warned the British government, "If any European power provokes war, we shall not shrink from it."

Similarly Seward advised Mercier that French recognition of the Confederacy would result in war with the United States. This nation might be defeated, he admitted bluntly, but France would know that she had been in a war. To William L. Dayton, the American Minister in Paris, Seward wrote: "Foreign intervention would oblige us to treat those who should yield it as allies of the insurrectionary party and to carry on the war against them as enemies. . . . The President and the people of the

United States deem the Union, which would then be at stake, worth all the cost and all the sacrifices of a contest with the world at arms, if such a contest should prove inevitable."

European interference meant war, but Seward offered the Old World powers the carrot as well as the stick. He reminded both Britain and France of their long tradition of friendship with the United States and assured them that this nation had cherished that peace. The American Republic, he instructed Adams, was "anxious to avoid all causes of misunderstanding with Great Britain; to draw closer, instead of breaking, the existing bonds of amity and friendship. There is nothing good or great," he added appealingly, "which both nations may not expect to attain or effect if they may remain friends. It would be a hazardous day for both branches of the British race when they should determine to test how much harm each could do the other." The Secretary extended similar assurances to the French: "We have no hostile or interested designs against any other state or nation whatever, and, on the contrary, we seek peace, harmony, and commerce with them all." Seward repeated ceaselessly his contention that the United States was one, and that the nations of Europe should not view themselves as neutrals between two imaginary belligerents in America, but as friends of the United States.

Seward's warnings were not without effect. When Lord Russell learned of the arrival in London of William L. Yancey, the Confederate Commissioner seeking recognition for his government, he wrote to Lyons in Washington: "If it can possibly be helped, Mr. Seward must not be allowed to get us into a quarrel. I shall see the southerners when they come, but unofficially and keep them at a proper distance." But even the unofficial reception of Yancey was too much for Seward. His next letter to Adams was so menacing that Lincoln revised certain passages and removed others. Nor would the President permit Adams to read the dispatch to Russell. Even in revised form the dispatch was little less than an ultimatum.

It suggested that Adams break off his relations with the British government if Russell persisted in seeing the Confederate Commissioner. Not content with this warning, Seward invited William Russell, the noted Washington correspondent of the London *Times,* to his home and read to him deliberately the long dispatch with its insinuations that Britain would destroy the American Republic if she could. Russell, he hoped, would not keep his impressions to himself.

Adams regarded the Secretary's warning as little less than a declaration of war. "I scarcely know how to understand Mr. Seward," he admitted. "The rest of the Government may be demented for all I know, but he surely is calm and wise." Adams informed Lord Russell in London that further relations between the British government and the "pseudo-commissioners" of the Confederate States, whether unofficial or not, would be regarded as a manifestation of hostility by the United States. Lord Russell did not receive the Southern Commissioner again. In May the British Minister announced a hands-off policy: ". . . we have not been involved in any way in that contest . . . and for God's sake, let us if possible, keep out of it.'"

Through Dayton, Seward informed the French Minister that the United States would regard any further communications of his government with the Southern Commissioners as "exceptional and injurious" to American dignity and honor. Even an unofficial reception of the emissaries of disunion, he complained, would give them encouragement to prosecute their effort to destroy the American Republic. Perhaps a warning would be sufficient to relieve the United States of further action, for Seward declared that this nation could not tolerate, whatever the consequences of its resistance, the recognition of the Confederacy by the French government.

Mercier and Lyons in Washington, still determined to commit their nations to a settlement of the American conflict, suggested mediation, with their governments serving as umpires between North and South. Lord Russell judiciously declined and Seward caused the diplomatic corps abruptly to drop what remained of the scheme. In a statement to the governor of Maryland he made it clear that the Federal government would accept no foreign arbitrament in settling its differences with the Confederacy. The American Constitution, he reminded the Europeans, provided all the required means for surmounting internal disorders. Arbitration would endanger the nation's integrity by substituting non-Constitutional devices for the normal functioning of the American system.

United States relations with Britain were unnecessarily disturbed in December, 1861, when Captain Charles Wilkes of the Federal warship *San Jacinto* stopped the British mail steamer *Trent* off the coast of Cuba and removed two Confederate leaders, James M. Mason and John Slidell. These men, among the South's ablest, had been dispatched to London and Paris respectively to replace the earlier commissioners. To the zealous Wilkes their capture was an unprecedented coup, but unfortunately he had broken the cherished maritime principle for which this nation supposedly had fought the British in the War of 1812. In London Henry Adams, son of the American Minister, saw the issue clearly, writing to his brother: "Good God, what's got into you all? What do you mean by deserting now the great principles of our fathers, by returning to the vomit of that dog Great Britain? What do you mean by asserting now principles against which every Adams yet has protested and resisted?"

Seward was embarrassed. He faced the necessity of satisfying the British who were wronged and at the same time of protecting American prestige abroad. "If I decide this case in favor of my own government," he admitted, "I must disavow its most cherished principles, and . . . forever abandon its essential policy. The country cannot afford the sacrifice. If I maintain those principles, and adhere to that policy, I must surrender the case itself." Seward soon decided on the latter course and conceded to the British with remarkable grace, for nowhere did the *Trent* case challenge his Union policies. "In coming to my conclusion," he wrote to Adams, "I have not forgotten that if the safety of this Union required the detention of the captured persons it would be the right and duty of this government to detain them. But the effective check and waning proportions of the existing insurrection, as well as the comparative unimportance of the captured persons themselves, when dispassionately weighed happily forbid me from resorting to that defense." Federal officials released the two Confederates promptly and sent them on their way. Lord Russell was relieved. He wrote, "I do not believe that Seward has any animosity to this country. It is all buncom."

What gave the South the presumption of success in its effort to secure European recognition was the alleged economic power of cotton. Southern writers in 1861 assumed that Britain would break the Northern blockade to guarantee the flow of cotton into England. "Cotton," declared the Charleston *Mercury,* "would bring England to her knees." *De Bow's Review* in June predicted that a blockade of the Southern ports would be "swept away by the English fleets of observation hovering on the Southern coasts, to protect English commerce, and especially the free flow of cotton to English and French factories." If cotton were king, the South had only to place an embargo on that commodity to force Britain to destroy the blockade. "Foreign nations will not recognize the independence of the Confederate States," admitted one Southern governor realistically, "until commerce with the Confederate States will become not only desirable, but necessary to their own prosperity." The Confederate Congress refused to establish an embargo, but Committees of Public Safety in the Southern seaport towns effectively halted the export of cotton to Europe.

By the spring of 1862 King Cotton had compelled neither Britain nor France to recognize Southern independence or break the blockade. Confederate efforts to force action in the British government by depriving Lancashire of raw cotton actually had the opposite effect. As one British leader observed, "I wonder the South do not see that our recognition *because* they keep cotton from us would be ignominious beyond measure, & that no English Parlt could do so base a thing." But the British resolve not to break the blockade resulted from a far more fundamental motive than a willingness to dispense with cotton, for the blockade defied America's own precedents and doctrines of neutral maritime rights. In undermining the principle of the Declaration of Paris that blockades to be binding must be effective, the United States was releasing England in a future conflict from this burdensome feature of the past. American action weakened the stand of the smaller maritime powers in their perennial effort to force Great Britain to recognize neutral rights in time of war.

Historians have agreed that cotton failed as a diplomatic weapon because Britain enjoyed too much lucrative trade with the North, requiring especially huge quantities of Northern grain, and because the textile workers most affected by the cotton famine remained staunch friends of the Union. Professor Ephraim D. Adams has accounted for the allegiance of English workingmen to Lincoln's wartime leadership by citing the general threat to democratic progress imposed by Southern secession. Either the North would triumph or democracy everywhere would be in jeopardy. The eventual Northern success vindicated the democratic system so completely, says Adams, that it led directly to the British Reform Bill of 1867.

Lincoln's Emancipation Proclamation, although designed, at least partially, to influence European attitudes toward the Union cause, had little effect on European sentiment and none on European action. British conservatives thought it foolhardy and anticipated a servile insurrection. Even William E. Gladstone was unmoved by Lincoln's action, reiterating his conviction that "negro emancipation cannot be effected, in any sense favourable either to black or to white by the bloody hand of war, especially of Civil War." British liberals, abolitionists, and workingmen lauded the Proclamation, but these groups had always favored the Union because it represented the cause of democracy. None of these groups, moreover, wielded influence over British policy. Northern diplomatic success found its fundamental explanation less in specific interests and doubts than in a great diplomatic tradition.

Europe's diplomatic tradition cautioned against any recognition of the Confederacy until the South had demonstrated the power required to establish and maintain its independence. Without the assurance of ultimate Southern success, European involvement would assume the risk of either an eventual ignominious retreat from a declared diplomatic objective or an unlimited military commitment to guarantee the achievement of Southern independence. Confronted with Europe's traditional realism, the Southern diplomatic cause in London and Paris could be no more successful than the Southern military cause in Virginia and Pennsylvania. Diplomacy reflects the status of power, and Southern power never appeared greater than during the summer and autumn months of 1862.

News of General George B. McClellan's retirement from before Richmond in the early summer of 1862 merely confirmed a general European conviction that the American Union was doomed. To European military experts, diplomats, and statesmen, Northern power seemed incapable of overcoming the defensive nature of the Southern military commitment. The North, Europe understood, enjoyed an immense industrial superiority, but the advantages of strategy, terrain, and leadership appeared to lie with the South. Confederate armies had no obligation to conquer the North, but only to beat off the Union forces. This they appeared capable of doing. In June, 1862, the London *Times* broached the issue of European intervention, convinced that Southern independence was inevitable. "It is plain," said the *Times,* that the time is approaching when Europe will have to think seriously of its relations to the two belligerents in the American war. . . . That North and South must now choose between separation and ruin, material and political, is the opinion of nearly every one who, looking impartially and from a distance on the conflict, sees what is hidden from the frenzied eyes of the

Northern politicians." Recognition of a successful cause could be both legitimate and effective.

For many British editors and politicians, McClellan's retreat from the peninsula during the summer of 1862 was like redemption. So dominant was the pro-Southern trend in British opinion that Henry Adams wrote from London, "There is no doubt that the idea here is as strong as ever that we must ultimately fail, and unless a very few weeks show some great military result we shall have our hands full in this quarter." Only a decisive Northern victory, he observed, could prevent European intervention. Public hostility, Charles Francis Adams wrote on July 18 to his son in America, was "rising every hour and running harder against us than at any time since the Trent affair." There was nothing to do but retreat. "I shut myself up," he lamented, "went to no parties and avoided contact with everyone except friends." Reports in the British press of the capture of McClellan's entire army, Adams believed, had been fabricated "to carry the House of Commons off their feet" as it commenced its crucial debate on William Shaw Lindsay's resolution calling for a more vigorous pro-Confederate British policy.

In defense of his resolution, Lindsay pointed to the inevitability of final separation between North and South. He declared that the Southern cause was just and that the North would now accept mediation. Lancashire was in distress. Lindsay quoted from a letter written by a mill hand, "We think it high time to give the Southern States the recognition they so richly deserve." Friends of the North were assured that the British Ministry would not be influenced by the parliamentary debate and therefore chose the strategy of permitting the pro-Confederates to wear themselves out against a stone wall of silence. After two days of verbal effort Lindsay asked for a postponement of his motion to "wait for king cotton to turn the screws still further." Somehow the debate created a strong impression in England that public opinion favored intervention.

That critical summer found the European diplomats confused and divided. Napoleon pondered the Southern victories, convinced that the moment for intervention had arrived. He informed the British Ministry that France would recognize Southern independence if the London government would follow. Edouard Antoine Thouvenel, the French Minister in Paris, did not share the Emperor's enthusiasm for intervention. He doubted that the French public had any interest in such involvement or that the Confederacy would win. He warned that French intervention, unless supported by both Britain and Russia, would result in an overcommitment of French power. Russia, he surmised, would reject every proposal for joint action. He was correct. Prince Gortchakov made it clear that his government would regard the dissolution of the Union as a catastrophe. In an interview with Bayard Taylor of the American Embassy in October, 1862, he said: "You know that the government of the United States has few friends among the Powers. England rejoices over what is happening to you; she longs and prays for your overthrow. France is less actively hostile; her interests would be less affected by the result; but she is not unwilling to see it. She is not your friend. . . . Russia, alone, has stood by you from the first, and will continue to stand by you. We are very, *very* anxious that some means should be adopted— that *any* course should be pursued—which will prevent the division which now seems inevitable."

In Washington Mercier, still counseling mediation, stood alone. Lyons had no interest in confronting Seward with that issue again. To Stoeckl he observed, "We ought not to venture on mediation unless we are ready to go to war." Lyons did not share the European hostility toward the American Union. During his visit to England in the summer of 1862 he wrote to the British chargé d'affaires in Washington, with reference to McClellan's defeat, "I'm afraid no one but me is sorry for it." He believed that the debate on British policy in Parliament was ill-timed. "I do not think we know here sufficiently the extent of the disaster [to McClellan] to be able to come to any conclusion as to what the European Powers should do," ran his warning. Stoeckl concluded that the ravages of war would prompt the North eventually to beg for mediation, but not yet. He doubted, moreover, that British or French recognition of the South would achieve anything. "It will not end the war and what is more," he predicted, "it will not procure cotton for them, and the distress of the manufacturing districts will not be lessened. It can be accomplished only by forcing open the Southern ports, thus leading to a clear rupture with the North."

In London Mason, misled by the public evidence of British interventionism and unmindful of the disturbing doubts in the Foreign Office, moved to drive home his apparent advantage. He dispatched a brief note to Lord Russell requesting an interview. This Russell refused, assuring Mason that no advantage would result from it. In a second dispatch the Confederate Commissioner phrased his position in great detail, but again Russell replied that the moment for recognition had not arrived. For Mason the official British position had suddenly become clear. The Ministry would not alter its policies until the South revealed its ability to gain and maintain its independence, and reports from America indicated that the South was faltering at New Orleans, Memphis, and Shiloh. From Vienna John Lothrop Motley observed with accuracy that diplomacy would continue to reflect the course of war in America.

In Paris Slidell met with equal opposition. Thouvenel convinced him that it would be unwise even to ask for recognition. France, he said, was involved in Italy, but Slidell understood clearly the cause for French hesitancy. To the Confederate government he wrote on August 24: "You will find by my official correspondence that we are still hard and fast aground here. Nothing will float us off but a strong and continued current of important successes in the field." England, he warned, would avoid intervention until the North and South had become entirely exhausted. "Nothing," he lamented, "can exceed the selfishness of English statesmen except their wretched hypocrisy. They are continually casting about their disinterested magnanimity and objection of all other considerations than those dictated by a high-toned morality, while their entire policy is marked by egotism and duplicity."

Despite the lack of conviction in Europe's judgment of Confederate prospects, Southern victories were prompting the British Ministry to consider intervention. Russell admitted that nothing less than further Confederate successes would force mediation on the North. "I think," he wrote to the Embassy in Washington, "we must allow the President to spend his second batch of 600,000 men before we can hope that he and his democracy will listen to reason." Russell was convinced privately that October, 1862, would be the anticipated time for action. Stonewall Jackson's victories in Virginia prompted him to inform Lord Palmerston, the Prime Minister, that "it really looks as if he might end the war." Palmerston agreed, writing on September 14: "The Federals . . . got a very complete smashing . . . even Washington or Baltimore may fall into the hands of the Confederates. If this should happen, would it not be time for us to consider whether in such a state of things England and France might not address the contending parties and recommend an arrangement upon the basis of separation." The British Cabinet awaited word from France.

Before Napoleon could commit France to intervention, the British government passed the moment of decision. The wise and respected British politican, Earl Granville, warned Russell that involvement would mean war. "I doubt," he cautioned, "if the war continues long after our recognition of the South, whether it will be possible for us to avoid drifting into it." If Granville's words lacked conviction, Northern arms did not. Before the end of September news reached London of McClellan's success at Antietam and Lee's retreat down the Shenandoah Valley. Russell, who had been the ministry's most vigorous spokesman for involvement, now admitted, "This American question must be well sifted." Palmerston's support of Russell's position had been conditioned on the Southern invasion of Maryland. Now on October 2 in a letter to Russell he also acknowledged the wisdom of Granville's argument. Since mediation would favor the Southern position, its acceptance in the North hinged on Southern triumphs. Ten days earlier the necessary conditions seemed impending; now Palmerston counseled delay. He had no interest in exposing Canada and British commerce to a war against the United States. Nor would he venture into a quarrel without the support of France and Russia. "The whole matter is full of difficulty," he concluded, "and can only be cleared up by some more decided events between the contending armies."

William E. Gladstone, Britain's liberal cabinet leader, continued to urge British involvement in the American conflict as a moral obligation. At Newcastle on October 7 he declared: "Jefferson Davis and the other leaders have made an army, they are making, it appears, a navy, and they have made what is more than either, they have made a nation." Gladstone denied that British mediation would be met by insult or war, for, he predicted in a memorandum to the Prime Minister, "America would feel the influence and weight of a general opinion on the part of civilized Europe that this horrible war ought to cease." Whatever the immediate Northern reaction, the British proposal would produce a powerful effect on opinion and alter affairs in America in favor of peace. But perhaps Gladstone was motivated by more than a moral revulsion to war. He had recently toured the North of England and was fearful that the unemployment in the cotton districts would produce a violent upheaval. By serving the cause of peace the great liberal might also serve the cause of the British cotton textile industry.

Palmerston, under pressure from the Cabinet, sought the advice of the Earl of Derby, leader of the opposition. Derby vigorously opposed both mediation and recognition. He reiterated the fundamental conviction of European conservatives that either action would merely irritate the North without advancing the cause of the South or procuring a single bale of cotton. Mediation, he added, would gain its apparent objective only if England were prepared to sweep away the blockade and invite a declaration of war

from the Lincoln administration. Intervention was hopeless because there was no way in which England could influence events in America short of military involvement.
Palmerston's decision reflected this fundamental reality.
Britain, he informed Lord Russell, "could take no step
nor make any communication of a distinct proposition with
any advantage." The North, he pointed out, demanded no
less than restoration of the Union and the South no less
than independence. To offer mediation would merely
pledge each party in the conflict more firmly to its uncom-
promising objective. Russell added his conviction that no
British action would be effective unless it were supported
by Russia, Prussia, Austria, and France. For nations of
such diverse interests agreement on interventionist policy
was impossible.

During the crucial months of October and November,
1862, Napoleon never disguised his sympathy for the
Confederate cause. But sentiment and policy are not
synonymous, and the French Emperor balked at involvement in the American conflict. He complained to Slidell
of troubles in Italy and Greece and acknowledged his fear
that if he acted alone England would desert him and
would attempt to embroil him in a war with the United
States. Slidell assured him that recognition would not be
regarded by the North as a *casus belli* and that with his
powerful navy he could defend French interests on the
seas without difficulty. To Slidell joint mediation was
worthless, for he had no faith in England or Russia.
Napoleon answered with a proposal acceptable to the
Southern Commissioner. France and Britain might seek
a six-month armistice in the American Civil War in the
interest of humanity. Napoleon's final program for joint
action was dispatched to both London and St. Petersburg.

In London the tripartite proposal threw the Cabinet into
confusion. Palmerston was displeased, for he no longer
had any interest in European intervention. Lord Russell
favored action provided European leaders could discover
terms upon which the warring sections in America would
agree. In lieu of this elusive formula he favored a Cabinet

discussion of the French dispatch. At the Cabinet meetings of November 11 and 12 Russell conceded the issue to Palmerston. Reported Gladstone to his wife: "The United States affair has ended and not well. Lord Russell rather turned tail. He gave way without resolutely fighting out his battle." In its reply to the French government, the British Ministry declared that mediation in any form was useless since Lincoln would not accept it.

At issue in the final Cabinet decision was the attitude of Russia. As early as November 8, St. Petersburg had informed the Foreign Office that the Russian government has rejected Napoleon's proposal. Prince Gortchakov advised the French that it was "essential to avoid the appearance of any pressure of a nature to offend American public opinion, and to excite susceptibilities very easily roused at the bare idea of intervention." Russell yielded on this key question to Palmerston when he wrote, "We ought not to move at present without Russia." Russia's inflexibility created the basis for a harmonious decision within the British Cabinet, and even Gladstone could write, "As to the state of matters generally in the Cabinet, I have never seen it smoother."

Throughout the months of decision in Europe, Seward exerted relentless pressure on the British and French governments. When Mercier transmitted a French offer of mediation to him in July, 1862, the Secretary warned that "the Emperor can commit no graver error than to mix himself in our affairs. At the rumor alone of intervention all the factions will reunite themselves against you and even in the border states you will meet resistance unanimous and desperate." It was not in the French interest, he continued to compromise the kindly feeling which the United States held for France. Mercier thereupon advised caution in Paris, adding that intervention could easily result in war. When Mercier apprised Seward of Europe's reaction to McClellan's withdrawal from Richmond, the Secretary again stormed back: "I have noticed it but as for us it would be a great misfortune if the powers should wish to intervene in our affairs. There is no possible compromise . . . and at any price, we will not admit the division of the Union." Seward acknowledged the kindly sentiments of Europe but replied that the best testimony of those sentiments would be Old World abstention from American affairs. When Mercier suggested that restoration of the Union was impossible, Seward told him: "Do not believe for a moment that either the Federal Congress, myself or any person connected with this government will in any case entertain any proposition or suggestion of arrangement or accommodation or adjustment from within or without upon the basis of a surrender of the Federal Union."

Above all Seward sought to disabuse European leaders of their conviction that a Northern victory was impossible. Nothing had occurred, he once wrote to Dayton in Paris, to shake the confidence of the Federal government in the ultimate success of its purpose. To those Europeans who insisted that the United States was too large for one nation, Seward retorted that it was too small for two. When Europe gave evidence of interventionist tendencies in August, 1862, Seward wrote to Adams: "The nation has a right and it is its duty, to live. Those who favor and give aid to the insurrection, upon whatever pretext, assail the nation in an hour of danger, and therefore they cannot be held or regarded as its friends. In taking this ground, the United States claim only what they concede to all other nations. No state can be really independent in any other position."

In denying Europe the right to intervene, Seward insisted that he was defending the principle of civil government itself, for at stake was nothing less than the existence of the United States. "Any other principle than this," he said, "would be to resolve government everywhere into a thing of accident and caprice, and ultimately all human society into a state of perpetual war." American policy was dictated by the law of self-preservation, and no nation, he added, "animated by loyal sentiments and inspired by a generous ambition can ever suffer itself to debate with parties within or without a policy of self-preservation."

Seward, therefore, instructed Adams not to debate, hear, or receive any communication from the British government which sought to advise the United States in its relations with the Confederacy. This nation was fighting for empire, he admitted in October, 1862, but it was an empire lawfully acquired and lawfully held. "Studying to confine this unhappy struggle within our own borders," he wrote to Dayton, "we have not only invoked no foreign aid or sympathy, but we have warned foreign nations frankly and have besought them not to interfere. We have practised justice towards them in every way, and concilia-tion to an unusual degree. But we are none the less determined for all that to be sovereign and to be free."

Seward's reaction to the British Cabinet debate of November revealed both confidence and dismay. It was not pleasant for a loyal American, he admitted to Adams, to observe an English cabinet discuss the future of the American Republic. But the United States, he added, en-joyed the right and possessed the power to determine its own destiny; never before was it better prepared to meet danger from abroad. The wheel of political fortune con-tinued to turn. England had once desired American friend-ship; she would do so again. "Neither politicians nor statesmen control events," the Secretary concluded. "They can moderate them and accommodate their ambitions to them, but they can do no more."

After November, 1862, all wartime diplomacy receded into insignificance. Whatever Southern hopes of European intervention still remained were shattered by the Con-federate disasters at Gettysburg and Vicksburg in July, 1863. In September Mason informed Russell by note that his mission had been terminated. The British Secretary replied coldly: "I have on other occasions explained to you the reasons which have inclined her Majesty's Govern-ment to decline the overtures you allude to. . . . These reasons are still in force, and it is not necessary to repeat them." Europe's final refusal to involve itself in the American struggle was nothing less than a total vindication of Seward's diplomacy. Whatever the North's diplomatic advantages, he had understood them and exploited them with astonishing effectiveness. He made it clear that any European nation which committed itself to the destruction of the American Union would pay dearly if it sought to fulfill that commitment.

In one sense there was nothing unique in the diplomatic issues raised by the American Civil War. Many nations in the past had undergone internal revolution in which elements seeking power had sought either to overthrow the established government or to establish the independence of some portion of its territory. Such uprisings had succeeded and failed, but when major power was involved they had demonstrated invariably that other nations, whatever their moral and material interests, really could not intervene diplomatically without running the risk of military involvement.

Unfortunately Union diplomacy after 1861 placed this nation in the unprecedented and embarrassing position of appearing to defy its own democratic principle of self-determination. Americans in the past, Europe recalled, had not only made declarations in favor of the Greek and Hungarian revolutions and applauded such revolutionary leaders as Louis Kossuth, but they had furnished them money for the declared purpose of assuring new disorders. Now Americans were compelled to recognize what they had often denied Europe—that governments cannot exist without authority and that, to maintain their authority, they must resort to force. Cassius Clay, to explain American purpose, once declared that the United States was fighting for nationality and liberty. To this the London *Times* replied sarcastically that it was difficult to understand how "a people fighting . . . to force their fellow citizens to remain in a confederacy which they repudiated, can be called the champions of liberty and nationalism." The Confederates were fighting for their independence, observed the *Times,* adding, "But with the Northerners all is different. They are not content with their own. They are fighting to coerce others."

Europe might have recalled that idealism had never established the official diplomatic tradition of the United States toward revolution and oppression. Whatever the concern of individual Americans toward events abroad, the nation's dictum since Washington's presidency had been one of abstention. John Quincy Adams had given it classical form in his Marcellus letters of 1794: "It is our duty to remain, the peaceful and silent, though sorrowful spectators of the European scene." Again in July, 1821, Adams declared that "America is the well-wisher to the freedom and independence of all. She is the vindicator only of her own." All national leaders prior to the Civil War, when holding positions of responsibility, agreed that any foreign intervention in behalf of liberal causes might well commit the United States beyond its national interest. President James Monroe recognized this when he refused to render aid to the revolting states of Latin America. They would receive recognition, he informed them, when they had demonstrated sufficient strength to establish their own independence. Palmerston was merely reflecting this diplomatic tradition when he admitted in October, 1862, that Britain "must continue merely to be lookers-on till the war shall have taken a more decided turn."

Tangible British and French interests were involved in the Southern struggle for independence, and to that extent neither nation could ignore events across the Atlantic. But until the South could demonstrate, as did the Latin American republics, that it could overcome the power and purpose of the North, European recognition would have defied one of the most significant and thoroughly established traditions of modern diplomacy. Except for one fleeting period in 1862, neither Britain nor France revealed any serious intention of breaking from their own past and assuming commitments which would endanger their territorial and commercial interests in the New World. Had Europe given expression to its moral sentiment by supporting the cause of the seemingly oppressed, it would merely have magnified the horror and confusion. Of this Seward left no doubt. He warned Europe in May, 1862, that its involvement in the affairs of the United States would not serve the interests of humanity. "If Europe will still sympathize with the revolution," he wrote, "it must now look forward to the end; an end in which the war ceases with anarchy substituted for the social system that existed when the war began. What will then have become of the interests which carried Europe to the side which was at once the wrong side and the losing one? Only a perfect withdrawal of all favor from the insurrection can now save those interests in any degree. The insurrectionary states, left hopeless of foreign intervention, will be content to stop in their career of self-destruction, and to avail themselves of the moderating power of the Federal government. If the nations of Europe shall refuse to see this, and the war must therefore go on to the conclusion I have indicated, the responsibility for that conclusion will not rest with the government of the United States."

Seward here touched the central issue of Europe's relationship to the conflict in America. If after the summer of 1862 it was still within the power of the Old World to bring injury to the North, it was beyond its power to bring salvation to the South. There were no inexpensive means available to Europe to achieve the liberation of the South against the North's determination to hold it. Those Europeans who sought to cast from the South the yoke of alien rule might have been moved by the moral sentiment of Gladstone, but they had no influence on Palmerston. And since the realities of power are always the determining factors in international affairs, a Gladstone in office, whatever his sentimentalism and faith in moral pressure, could have influenced the internal affairs of the United States, wrapped in civil war, with no more success than the masters of *Realpolitik* who rejected such purpose as a matter of principle.

Died of Democracy

David Donald

HISTORIANS HAVE EXPLAINED Confederate defeat in a variety of ways, but even as they blame the South's weaker economic resources, declining morale, defective strategy, and feeble political leadership, they have a faintly apologetic air. They know that, had the Confederacy gained its independence, they would be writing, with equal cogency, to explain the Southern victory. The historian, in other words, is a camp follower of the successful army.

As the historian explains why the winning side triumphed, he naturally tends to identify the victor with the most cherished values of the society in which he lives. He may describe the defeated cause as courteous, chivalrous, and romantic (maternal virtues which we admire but do not respect), but he attributes to the victor the masculine traits of strength, power, aggressiveness, and tough-mindedness (paternal assets which we may not like but necessarily respect). In American society there are three such values to which historians give adherence: All are convinced that it is a desirable and necessary thing to preserve the American Union; all believe that Negro slavery is an evil; and all profess a faith in democratic government.

It is not the truth of these beliefs but their juxtaposition which causes the great confusion about the Civil War. Historians, recognizing that Lincoln's government was fighting for the preservation of the Union and for the freedom of the slaves, attribute to it also the third great positive value, the defense of democracy. Such a view is a distortion of the facts. If we could free ourselves of the notion that democracy (a "good" thing) must inevitably have been connected with the winning (hence "good") Lincoln government, we would discover abundant evidence that

79

the Confederacy, not the Union, represented the democratic forces in American life.[1]

The democratic tendencies of the Confederacy were all too plainly reflected in its army. Accustomed to regarding themselves as the equals of any men in the world, the Southerners never took kindly to regimented life. Even their appearance showed that they considered themselves individualistic citizens who were temporarily assisting their country. One astonished Englishman, after seeing his first Confederate soldiers, gasped: "Anything less like the received notion, at home, of how a soldier should look . . . never met my eye."

Like all American soldiers in all wars, the Confederate disliked military discipline. Mississippi volunteers shirked assignments which they found tedious, declaring "they did not enlist to do guard duty but to fight the Yankies." At the outbreak of the war, when wealthier soldiers received onerous orders, some coolly instructed their Negro servants to carry them out, meanwhile uncomplainingly taking "upon themselves the duty of sitting on the fence and superintending the work." Others hired substitutes to perform their chores. "The two or three men of the overseer class who were to be found in nearly every company," George Cary Eggleston recalled, "turned some nimble quarters by standing other men's turns of guard-duty at twenty-five cents an hour."

The Southern soldier reserved his democratic right to interpret his orders broadly. The British observer, Colonel J. A. L. Fremantle, at first thought Confederate sentries "quite as strict as, and ten times more polite than, regular soldiers" because they efficiently challenged him when he entered James Longstreet's camp. But when he complimented the Confederate commander, Longstreet "replied,

[1] I am using "democracy" in this essay precisely as Alexis de Tocqueville used it in Democracy in America; it includes not merely such political manifestations as the extension of the suffrage, but all antiauthoritarian, individualistic, "levelling" tendencies in nineteenth-century American society.

laughing, that a sentry, after refusing you leave to enter a camp, might very likely, if properly asked, show you another way in, by which you might avoid meeting a sentry at all."

Southern soldiers simply disobeyed orders which they deemed unreasonable. Unconvinced that it was necessary to carry heavy packs, they carelessly tossed irreplaceable equipment aside on long, hot marches. Even the idea of marching at a regular rate in tidy lines offended their sense of individuality. "Our great embarrassment," Robert E. Lee reported to Jefferson Davis, "is the reduction of our ranks by straggling, which it seems impossible to prevent. . . . Our ranks are very much diminished—I fear from a third to one-half of our original numbers."

The Southern soldiers who volunteered at the outbreak of the war considered it their right to determine for themselves the length of their service. After a victorious battle in the early days of the war "many would coolly walk off home, under the impression that they had performed their share." When Jefferson Davis attempted to construct a more stable army through conscription, he probably lost more than he gained. "This Conscript Act will do away with all the patriotism we have," an indignant South Carolinian wrote in April, 1862, "A more oppressive law was never enacted in the most uncivilized country or by the worst of despots." Other Southern soldiers expressed their resentment by deserting in droves.

Unwilling to have their liberties curtailed by the Confederate government, Southern soldiers were also heartily opposed to undemocratic exercise of authority by their officers. They obeyed orders on the battlefield, but they saw no reason why officers should give themselves special airs in camp. Privates both resented and envied the privileges which officers enjoyed. The common soldier had "the hardships to undergo," a hungry Alabaman complained, while the officers had "bacon to eat, sugar to put in their coffee and all luxuries of this kind." An Englishman reported that he had never heard such handsome cursing as when Confederate privates, off duty and "squatted cross-legged on beds," spent their evenings damning their superiors' "eyes and limbs."

Often the Confederate soldiers were in a position to put their officers in their places. Sometimes they petitioned for the resignation of unpopular commanders; occasionally they rode an especially objectionable officer on a rail until he promised better behavior. Chiefly, however, the Confederate privates relied for redress upon their sovereign democratic right to elect their own officers. The elective system, a carry-over from the old peacetime militia, seemed perfectly reasonable to these democratic individualists. The theory behind it, as Eggleston remarked, was "that the officers were the creatures of the men, chosen by election to represent their constituency in the performance of certain duties, and that only during good behavior."

Though professional military men unanimously disapproved of the election of officers, politicians, sensitive to the democratic aspirations of the Southern fighting man, fought to continue the system. Southern soldiers "are not automatons," a Confederate congressman insisted, "dancing to the turning of some official organ grinder. The best *mind* and the best *blood* in the country are in the army, and much of both are found in the ranks. They have not lost the identity of the citizen in the soldier." Even Jefferson Davis agreed: "The citizens of the several States volunteered to defend their homes and inherited rights . . . the troops were drawn from the pursuits of civil life. Who so capable to judge of fitness to command a company, a battalion or a regiment as the men composing it?"

The result of the elective system was further to demoralize Confederate discipline. The men spent much of their time in quasi-political campaigning. "Authorize a squad of six men to elect a Lance Corporal," one observer commented, "and five of the number will at once become candidates." Secretary of War James A. Seddon pointed out that the elective system inevitably produced "an undue regard to popularity, especially among the non-commissioned officers, and a spirit of electioneering subversive of subordination and discipline." An Alabama congressman agreed: "I have seen a company rendered inefficient for months because of the opportunity of exercising the elective franchise in the choice of a lieutenant."

Of course the Confederacy was not alone in having these problems of discipline. Billy Yank was in most ways astonishingly like Johnny Reb, and both Civil War armies were, by modern standards, shockingly disorganized and maladministered. Yet in the Northern armies the respect for soldiers' individual rights never quite led to chaos. For one thing, the Lincoln government moved much more speedily to end the system of electing officers. What is more important, the Union administration had at its disposal two sizable reserves of manpower, neither of which had much experience in democracy nor much tendency toward individualism. The Federal armies recruited heavily from European immigrants. By 1864 one out of every four or five Union soldiers was of European birth, many of them newly arrived immigrants. Relatively uncontaminated by American notions of democracy or individualism, they were prepared to serve in a regular and subordinate fashion in the Union armies.

At the same time Federal enrolling officers were recruiting Negroes. By 1865 the Union army included 178,895 colored soldiers—roughly five times the number of men in Lee's army when he surrendered at Appomattox. These "Negroes make good soldiers," a lieutenant in one of the colored regiments wrote home to his wife. "They are docile and quick to learn . . . and they have a decided advantage over our white soldiers in the fact that they are taught *obedience* to every command, especially when that command comes from a white man. The trouble with *our* [white] volunteers, is, that they have always been accustomed to do as they pleased and to have their own way about everything and it is very hard work to come under the yoke of army discipline. With the Negro it is right the reverse."

Foreign observers almost invariably commented that the Union army was a far less colorful and interesting aggregation than that of the Confederacy. So it was, but it was also a far better organized and disciplined fighting force. The Southern soldier was a democratic, liberty-loving individualist; his Union counterpart became a cog in a vast machine.

The Confederacy's tolerance of democracy was not confined to military affairs. In civil rights, too, the South had an astonishingly libertarian record. Though engaged in deadly war, Davis' government preserved the traditional civil rights of freedom of speech, freedom of the press, and freedom from arbitrary arrest, even when the government itself was debilitated by these rights.

Let no one romantically conclude that the Southern government permitted criticism and dissent because all its people were loyally united behind the lost cause. Quite the contrary. Both Davis and his government were subjected to tirades of abuse. Davis, said T. R. R. Cobb of Georgia, was "the embodiment and concentration of cowardly littleness [which] he garnishes over with pharasaical hypocrisy. How can God smile upon us while we have such a man [to] lead us." The editor of the influential Richmond *Examiner*, E. A. Pollard, described Davis as "a literary dyspeptic who had more ink than blood in his veins, an intriguer, busy with private enmities." Robert Toombs, the Confederacy's first Secretary of State, declared: "Davis's incapacity is lamentable. . . ." The Vice-President of the Confederacy, Alexander H. Stephens, announced that Davis was simultaneously "weak and vascillating [*sic*], timid, petulant, peevish, obstinate, but not firm." "How God has afflicted us with a ruler!" exclaimed Linton Stephens, the Vice-President's brother, a leader in the Georgia House of Representatives. "He is a *little, conceited, hypocritical, snivelling, canting, malicious, ambitious, dogged,* knave and fool."

Not one of these, nor any of the other critics, of the Confederate President had his liberty of utterance impaired. Davis was well aware of the enmity of his critics and thought that most Southern newspapers were partisan nd venal; Lee scathingly remarked that, from the tone of he press, the Confederacy had "put all our worst generals o commanding our armies, and all our best generals to diting newspapers"—but neither man did anything to urb the Southerners' limitless democratic right of free xpression. "When Davis's advisers were to urge that anti-Administration papers be restrained, he would not hear of t," Hudson Strode points out. "As a democrat, he believed n maintaining complete freedom of the press." It is true hat in January, 1862, the Confederate Congress did pass a law forbidding the publication of unauthorized news of roop movements, but even this slight regulation was bit-erly protested and flagrantly ignored. No Southern news->aper was ever suppressed by the Confederate government or its opinions, however critical or demoralizing. The ardent wish of Secretary of War George W. Randolph was realized: that "this revolution may be . . . closed without .uppression of one single newspaper in the Confederate States."

More significant militarily was the Confederacy's in-istence upon maintaining the cherished legal rights of reedom from arbitrary arrest and upon preserving due >rocess of law. This sentiment was so strong that, though he Confederacy was invaded and Richmond was actually endangered, President Davis did not dare institute martial aw until he had received the permission of his Congress. While General George B. McClellan was about to assault he Confederate capital in 1862, the Southern Congress lebated the question and concluded that their President was "subject to the Constitution and to the laws enacted >y Congress in pursuance of the Constitution. He can exert no power inconsistent with law, and, therefore, he cannot declare martial law." Grudgingly Congress per-mitted Davis to suspend the privilege of the writ of habeas corpus for three brief periods—once when McClellan was within sight of Richmond, again during the Fredericks->urg-Chancellorsville threat, and once more when Grant was pushing through the Wilderness. Even then he was allowed to suspend the writ only in limited areas, not throughout the Confederacy. When he came to Congress for a renewal of his authority during the grim winter of 1864–1865, he was refused, lest too much power in the hands of a dictatorial president curb the democratic rights of the people.

The result, of course, was that disloyal elements throughout the South had almost unrestricted freedom. If a member of the Peace and Constitution Society, the Order of Heroes, or any of the other disloyal bands that centered in the hill country of the South was arrested, he was tried by civil process before a jury of his peers—many of whom probably belonged to the same disloyal organization as himself. The influential Confederate bored with army service could often secure from a judge of his own persuasion a writ of habeas corpus, which released him from military duty. The planter who hoarded grain, the merchant who traded with the enemy, the blockade-runner who brought in laces and perfumes rather than desperately needed medicines—all were equally secure. And when Davis reluctantly considered cracking down on these disloyal elements, a newspaper controlled by his own Vice-President came out with a black-bordered edition, as if in mourning, and exclaimed: "Georgians, behold your chains!—Freemen of a once proud and happy country, contemplate the last act which rivets your bonds and binds you hand and foot, at the mercy of an unlimited military authority."

Again, one does not suggest that the North was free from these troubles of disloyalty and sedition, nor should he imply that the Lincoln government handled them with the same grim efficiency which was shown during the later Woodrow Wilson and Franklin D. Roosevelt administrations. Yet, in comparison with the Confederacy, the Union government did curtail civil liberties. As soon as the fighting started, President Lincoln, without delaying to consult Congress, suspended the privilege of the writ of habeas corpus, at first for a small area in the East, later for the entire nation. At a subsequent date he reported his *fait accompli* to Congress: "These measures, whether strictly legal or not, were ventured upon, under what appeared to be a popular demand, and a popular necessity; trusting then, as now that Congress would readily ratify them." Congress had little choice but to ratify, and the disloyal citizen no alternative but to acquiesce. At least 15,000 civilians were imprisoned in the North for alleged disloyalty or sedition. They were arrested upon a presidential warrant and were kept incarcerated without due process of law. It did the disaffected citizen no good to go to court for a writ of habeas corpus to end his arbitrary arrest. On orders from President Lincoln himself, the military guard imprisoning him refused to recognize a judicial writ even when it came from Chief Justice Roger B. Taney.

Freedom of the press was also seriously abridged in the North. To be sure, Northern editors abused President Lincoln as "a slang-whanging stump speaker," a "half-witted usurper," a "mole-eyed" monster with "soul . . . of leather," "the present turtle at the head of the government," of "the head ghoul at Washington"—but they did so at the acknowledged risk of having their papers suppressed and going to prison. Over three hundred Northern newspapers were suppressed, for varying periods, because they opposed the administration's policies or favored stopping the war.

But in painting this picture one must be careful not to exaggerate. If, as J. G. Randall noted, "Legally the Civil War stands out as an eccentric period, a time when constitutional and legal restraints did not fully operate and when the 'rule of law' at least partially broke down," one must also add that "civil liberties were not annihilated" and "the traditional attachment of the American people to the 'rule of law' as a principle had its steadying effect." Lincoln was no dictator. He disliked the arbitrary procedures which he felt compelled to employ, and he carefully used them for no selfish or self-promoting purpose. Furthermore, few Nothern citizens were affected by these curbs on civil rights. Enthusiastic in their support of the Union cause, most neither knew nor cared that freedom of the press was abridged or that arbitrary arrests were numerous. Yet the test of civil liberties is not the freedom of the majority but that of the dissenter. In the Confederacy the dissenter retained his democratic rights down to Appomattox.

Political democracy, too, was unimpaired in the Confederacy. Jefferson Davis took care to abridge no Southerner's political rights. Elected provisional president through no solicitation of his own, re-elected as the first—and only—regular President of the Confederacy, Davis did not believe that he should interfere in politics, either to solicit votes for his friends or to win support for his measures. Davis' political record as president is almost exclusively negative. He endorsed no congressional candidates, and he discouraged the formation of political parties in the South. When North Carolina held a critical gubernatorial election in 1864 to choose between Zebulon Vance, pledged to sustain the war effort, and William W. Holden, dedicated to withdrawing the state from the Confederacy and making an independent peace, Davis expressed no public preference between the candidates. Nor did he make any attempt to secure the defeat of Governor Joseph E. Brown, of Georgia, though Brown, with the backing of Vice-President Stephens, did all he could to hamstring the Richmond government, announced that the people must check Davis' "fearful strides towards a centralized government with unlimited powers," and urged a convention of the "sovereign, equal, and independent states" to make peace with the Union. Davis did not try to replace his arch-rival, Stephens. In the South, the soldiers knew it was wartime, but not the politicians.

The record of the Lincoln government is in marked contrast. Lincoln regularly used patronage to build up a political machine, dedicated to supporting his policies. At first he tried not to intervene in the elections themselves, but his hands-off policy, comparable to that pursued by Davis, resulted in a disastrous defeat for the Republican party in the congressional elections of 1862. The key states of New York, Pennsylvania, Ohio, Indiana, and Illinois were lost to the Democrats. The newly-elected Democratic legislators in those states began condemning the Lincoln administration for catering to the Negro and for ruthlessly kidnapping white citizens, who were "cast into dungeons . . . to remain, sicken and die." They announced: "War alone is no remedy for the evil of disunion."

Rapidly Lincoln moved to reverse his policy by strengthening the hands of his friends. When Republican Governor O. P. Morton of Indiana was faced in 1863 with a hostile Democratic majority in the state legislature, which threatened to curb his appointing powers and his control of the state militia, the Republicans, by prearrangement, walked out of the chamber, leaving the legislature without a quorum and unable to transact any business. The Democrats then adjourned the session, believing that Morton, in order to carry on the government, must call them promptly back. Instead, the Indiana governor made a flying trip to Washington, saw Lincoln and Secretary of War E. M. Stanton, and returned to Indianapolis bearing $250,000 extracted from war department funds, on which he ran the state government until the next election, blithely ignoring constitutional regulations and majority rule.

Having learned a lesson from 1862, Lincoln was prepared to take a more active, preventive role in the presidential election two years later. When he saw that the Northwestern states were going to show a closely balanced vote, he wrote in September, 1864, to General W. T. Sherman, whose army was in a tight spot before Atlanta: "Any thing you can safely do to let [your] soldiers, or any part of them, go home to vote at the State election, will be greatly in point." Although Lincoln added that "this is, in no sense, an order," he was clearly giving a directive, and it was one which Sherman promptly obeyed. The Republicans carried the Northwest by narrow majorities. In Pennsylvania, too, the Democrats were threatening, and it was found possible to furlough several thousands from Grant's army before Richmond. Not all the soldiers were Republicans, to be sure—but Democratic soldiers found it strangely difficult to secure furloughs.

In 1864 a number of Northern states permitted their

soldiers to vote in the field. Republican canvassers were afforded every facility for getting to the front, but Democratic politicians were often harassed by long delays in Washington. Lincoln himself took a great interest in the soldier vote. When Secretary of War Stanton gruffly refused, on grounds of military security, to disclose the location of New York regiments to the official canvassers from the Empire State, they complained to the President, who at once interceded in their behalf. When they commented on the alacrity with which the President had overruled his Secretary, E. B. Washbourne, an old friend from Lincoln's Illinois period, explained the facts of life: "Why that would beat Mr. Lincoln. You don't know him. While he is a great statesman, he is also the keenest of politicians alive. If it could be done in no other way, the president would take a carpet bag and go round and collect those votes himself."

The collapse of the Confederacy, then, came not from deficient economic resources, insufficient manpower, defective strategy, or weak political leadership. All of these were handicaps; but none was fatal. The real weakness of the Confederacy was that the Southern people insisted upon retaining their democratic liberties in wartime. If they were fighting for freedom, they asked, why should they start abridging it? As soldiers, as critics of their government, and as voters they stuck to their democratic, individualistic rights. In the administration of the Southern army, in the management of Southern civilian affairs, and in the conduct of Southern political life, there is, then, extensive evidence that we should write on the tombstone of the Confederacy: "Died of Democracy."

Jefferson Davis and the Political Factors in Confederate Defeat

David M. Potter

THE QUESTION "Why did the North win the Civil War?" is only half of a question by itself, for the other half is "Why did the South lose the Civil War?" Was one side more crucial than the other? Did the North win because the South was a natural loser, or did the South lose because the North was a natural winner? Is one side of a watch crystal concave because the other is convex, or is one convex because the other is concave? Shall we explain the results in terms of what the North did to the South, as Kenneth P. Williams tended to do in *Lincoln Finds a General,* or in terms of what the South failed to do to the North, as Douglas S. Freeman tended to do in his studies of *R. E. Lee* and *Lee's Lieutenants?*

The answer to these questions is easier in theory than it is in application. In principle it is clear that the outcome of a contest between two parties results not from the qualities of either taken alone, but from the differentials between them. Yet to measure these differentials, one must give a kind of bifocal attention to both parties at the same time. This is an ambidextrous feat which historians of the Confederacy and historians of the Union have alike found hard to attain. Consequently, most of the answers come to us in terms of the strength of the Union or the weakness of the Confederacy, rather than of the relative qualities of the two.

Where differentials are examined, they can be measured more precisely in economic terms than in any other, and historians have long been impressed by the great economic superiority of the North. Here there are innumerable measurements—of manpower, of wealth, of railroad mileage, of industrial capacity—all of which point up the overwhelming advantage on the side of the Union. These comparisons have led many writers to conclude that the Sout was fighting against the census returns and that Norther victory was inevitable from the beginning.

One-sided as these statistical comparisons are, even the fail to reveal in full the economic handicaps of the South No statistics can measure, for instance, how much th Confederacy suffered from the fact that it had the kind c economy that is prostrated by war, in contrast to the Unio which had the kind of economy that flourishes under wa time conditions. War invigorated the Northern econom by stimulating a leading form of Northern economic activ ity, namely industrial production. Thus the conflict brough prosperity to the civilian population, and civilian moral remained good largely because civilians had nothing to b demoralized about. But in the Confederacy, war paralyze the chief form of economic activity, which was the cu tivation of cotton. As the flow of income from cotton drie up, the economy languished, the economic welfare c civilians suffered, and their morale deteriorated. In th end, the economic morale of the people collapsed befor their military morale was exhausted.

In terms of economic logic, it can perhaps be demon strated that the Confederacy, hopelessly overmatched b almost every measure of strength, was doomed to defea But history not only shows that in war the lighter antagonis sometimes defeats the heavier, it also shows that wha seems logically certain often fails to happen. Thus, if w survey the course of the Civil War, do we not find that, i actuality, the Confederacy developed very formidabl striking power—power impressive enough to make Lin coln doubt, even as late as 1864, that the Union woul be saved? Do we not find the effective power of the op posing forces balanced so evenly that sometimes great re sults seemed to swing on the hinge of relatively trivia events? If a Confederate soldier had not shot Stonewa Jackson in the dusk at Chancellorsville, if Gouverneu Warren had not had a quick eye for Little Round Top if a duplicate copy of Lee's plan of campaign in September 1862, had not been used by someone on D. H. Hill's stat to wrap three cigars, might not a delicate balance have swung the other way in spite of all the statistics?

In weighing the question whether inescapable forces doomed the South in advance, it is well also to remember that the question is not what the South might have done during the last twenty-one months of the forty-eight-month war. For in fact, the result had been registered after Gettysburg and perhaps even after Sharpsburg, and all the South could hope for then was that the Northern people might fail to notice that they had won—as indeed the Northern Democrats did fail to notice in the election campaign of 1864. But for fourteen months before Lee came to high command, and for perhaps thirteen months after he did so, the result often appeared to be in real doubt, and it seems legitimate to question whether more effective political policies by the Confederates might at that time have made a crucial difference.

If the balance was, in fact, a delicate one, the analysis of forces must go far beyond the *à priori* arguments of economic determinism. While no one will deny that economic factors gave to the North an immense advantage, the precise question is whether other countervailing factors could possibly have offset it. For instance, could superior military and political skill on the Confederate side have done so? Reducing this question still further: Was there a differential in military performance in favor of the South which tended to offset, in part, the economic differential in favor of the North? The preponderance of historical opinion has agreed that the answer to this question is yes. For four long years, Lee's army did stave off defeat. But was the differential in political performance also in favor of the South? If it was, then one can say that Southern military and political prowess were hopelessly overmatched by the Union's sheer economic weight. But unless the effectiveness of the Confederate government equalled or surpassed that of the Union government, we cannot rest the evaluation of Confederate policy, as some historians have done, with the affirmation that Confederate leaders should not be blamed for their mistakes since the problems that they faced were insuperable. Instead, we shall have to say that economic and political factors, in conjunction, produced the final result, despite military factors which had a contrary tendency. Can we not go a step farther and ask whether the difference between Union and Confederate political performance was not as great as or greater than the economic disparities—whether in fact, the discrepancy in ability between Abraham Lincoln and Jefferson Davis was not as real and as significant as the inequality in mileage between Union and Confederate railroad systems?

The danger of a question like this is that it tends to displace one explanation with another, and to minimize the truly immense handicaps of the Confederacy. No just appraisal would ever underestimate the dead weight of those handicaps, but on the other hand, an appreciation of the magnitude of the South's problems should not stand in the way of a recognition that Confederate policy sometimes aggravated these problems instead of diminishing them, and that mistakes of policy as well as the handicaps of given conditions weakened the Southern cause.

In a number of the situations in which the Confederacy failed, it is fairly evident both that the problems were essentially insurmountable and also that government policy made them even worse than they would otherwise have been. In the matter of raising public revenue and controlling inflation, for instance, it was inevitable that a new government with no gold reserves and no revenue laws would face financial crisis, and also that the scarcity of goods in a blockaded, nonindustrial country would cause an inflationary rise in prices. But while no government could have wholly averted these evils, almost any government could have done more than the Confederacy did. Hesitating to resort to taxation, it called on the states for funds, and they met the requisitions largely by borrowing. In the end, only about one per cent of Confederate revenue was raised by taxation, which is a smaller proportion than any modern government in wartime has raised in this way. In spite of this abuse, the Confederate dollar held up almost as well as the Union greenback during the first two years of the war, which suggests that a sounder financial policy might have sustained it somewhat longer.

A similar combination of unavoidable difficulties on the one hand, and mistaken choices between policy alternatives on the other appears in the treatment of what had traditionally been the South's major economic asset—namely the cotton crop. In 1861, this asset was worth $225 million in gold, or nearly ten times as much as the actual gold supply in the Confederacy. Every one of the 4,500,000 bales, if exported and held in a European warehouse, would have helped to pay for vital Confederate purchases overseas. The loss of a considerable part of this value was inevitable, because shipping could not have been procured to export the whole crop before the Union blockade became operative. It was fantastic to suppose, for instance, as did Alexander H. Stephens, that fifty iron-bottomed boats could have been bought and used for the export of 4,000,000 bales. But while lack of shipping forced the Confederate leaders to keep a part of the cotton at home, they willingly embraced a fallacious belief—the King Cotton delusion—which caused them voluntarily to keep all of it at home. This belief that, by withholding their cotton, they would force Britain and France to intervene in the war, failed to face up to the question whether there were commodities which the Confederacy would need even more urgently than Britain and France would need cotton fibres.

There were realistic men in the Confederacy who perceived the fallacy in the cotton policy. As early as April, 1861, Secretary of the Treasury C. G. Memminger resolutely opposed the cotton embargo and expressed his disapproval "of any obstruction to commerce in our ports." During 1862, the Commissary Department faced the reality that supplies were vital and must be procured even if it meant trading cotton to the enemy—a far more serious matter than selling it abroad. According to R. G. H. Kean, in November, Commissary General Lucius B. Northrop reported that "he could not supply the Army unless allowed to purchase bacon from the enemy at Memphis with cotton," and the Quartermaster General wanted to procure blankets in the same way. The Secretary of War, George W. Randolph, had already become convinced of the necessity of a cotton trade limited to the bureau in question. By April, 1863, Secretary of State Judah P. Benjamin broke sharply away from the King Cotton doctrine, asserted that it was a matter of primary importance to bring in army supplies at Confederate ports, and proposed a definite export of cotton "to be received by the merchant vessels of France at certain designated points." Before the end of the war, even General Lee strongly recommended to President Davis that the trade which was already bringing New York bacon to his army should be widely extended to secure other supplies.

These men perceived the point of a problem posed by Kean: "The question is simply whether they [the North or the British and French] suffer more for the . . . cotton . . . or we for the indispensable articles of salt, meat, clothing, medicines." But Kean also reported, "The President resisted it [the proposal for trade] in toto." In March, 1863, he noted in his diary that "the President has yielded at last on the subject of getting meat from the enemy for cotton"—this in connection with Generaly Kirby Smith's trade at the mouth of the Río Grande. But Kean added, "Too late to do much good." Nearly a year later, he was still criticizing Davis for placing upon the cotton trade, restrictions which made it almost impossible to conduct. As he reported, regulations for the trade were drawn very carefully in the War Office, and sent to the President, but "they came back so modified as to destroy the trade by their stringency."

In the end, cotton responded to the laws of necessity, and a vast amount was traded through the lines. In fact, this trade became an important factor in sustaining the armies in the West, and Memphis took its place as "a greater outfitting point for Confederate armies than Nassau." Private families—even patriotic ones—found that by smuggling out a single bale they might escape starvation, while quartermasters and commissaries and state officials learned that this was sometimes the only way to keep Southern armies in the field. Therefore, it cannot be said that Jefferson Davis succeeded in imposing a policy based upon the King Cotton doctrine. All that he did succeed in doing was to reduce the cotton situation to chaos. In this chaos, the Confederate government lacked control of the cotton in the South and lacked a constructive overall policy for utilizing such cotton as it did control. Consequently, private owners smuggled large amounts of cotton through the lines, thus breaking the partial embargo, demoralizing the citizens who were too patriotic to smuggle, and creating competition against their own government in bidding for the goods which cotton would buy. At the same time, the government itself survived by accepting, more or less unwittingly, the fruits of a trade conducted mostly on an unsanctioned basis by desperate or imaginative minor officials. But while permitting enough trade to break its own embargo, the government never faced the question how best to reap the potential advantage of the cotton supply as a whole. At the end of the war, 2,500,000 bales had been destroyed to prevent them from falling into the hands of the enemy; less than 1,000,000 probably had been exported through the blockade; and an incalculable amount had been smuggled through the lines, more for the gain of private parties than for the good of the cause. Such was the ultimate destiny of what everyone recognized as the greatest economic asset of the Confederacy.

The same pattern of initial handicaps compounded by mistaken policy appears in the procurement of supplies and foodstuffs for the Confederate Army. The initial handicap lay in the fact that there were many commodities, especially those produced abroad, which were inevitably scarce, or even unobtainable. The mistaken policy lay in the fact that even the goods which might have been produced in sufficient quantity became scarce because of restrictive economic measures. In this connection, it is important to recognize that, as the war developed, Southern farmers turned from the production of cotton to the production of grain, and there was no overall deficiency of food. But in procuring food for the army the Confederacy found itself in the dilemma that if it purchased supplies on the open market at an uncontrolled price, inflation would mushroom, while on the other hand, if it requisitioned supplies at an arbitrary price, productive output would be discouraged and the loyalty of the producers would be impaired. Caught between these alternatives, the government chose to give priority to avoiding inflation. Accordingly it set up a system of impressment, which partook of legalized confiscation, since it permitted military officers to seize draft animals or foodstuffs at a fixed price which was sometimes less than half of the market value. The net result of this was to encourage corrupt practices, to place civilian morale under an almost intolerable strain, and to discourage production without noticeably slowing the pace of inflation. As men either hoarded their crops, or stopped planting altogether, severe shortages developed. By March, 1863, these shortages were so acute that Kean wrote: "The Army will be starved and famine will ensue in the cities unless the Secretary changes his policy and buys in the market for the best price. The government will have to outbid the traders; else *neither* will get anything of the present scanty stock and no future stock will be produced."

The failures of the impressment system have received full recognition at the hands of historians, but another error in economic mobilization, which has largely escaped notice, was the failure of the Confederacy to assert control over the use of a labor force which constituted more than one-third of its manpower—namely that part which consisted of Negro slaves. Where manpower was white, the government did not hesitate very many months before adopting conscription laws which made the allocation of the labor of such men subject to public control. These laws drew most men of military age into the army, but they left others, whose occupations were deemed to be essential, in a civilian status. But where manpower was Negro, conscription did not bring it under similar control. Because of the *idée fixe* that slaves were property and not persons, the allocation of nearly 40 per cent of the Confederacy's total manpower was left to the whim and discretion of individual slaveholders. This produced great inequalities of sacrifice, for manpower meant earning power on the farms. Conscription had taken the manpower, and thus the earning power of the nonslaveholding families, who suffered great privations during the war. It left most of the manpower and thus the earning power of the slaveholding families, whose privations were usually much less severe.

It is an ironical comment on the blind refusal of the South to regard slaves as men that when resentment flared up against this system, it took the form of protest not against the failure to conscript slaves—whether for military or nonmilitary service—but against the exemption from military service of one white man as overseer for every twenty slaves whose labor had to be supervised. The disgruntled men who said bitterly that this was "a rich man's war and a poor man's fight," resented deeply the fact that a limited number of white men were allowed to remain in noncombatant employment as overseers, yet they apparently did not resent at all the fact that the labor of several million black workers continued to be used for the benefit of their owners, while the labor of white workers was subject to the demands of the Confederacy. The failure to include Negroes in any overall system of public allocation of labor was both a fundamental source of inequality of sacrifice on the part of the people and a basic flaw in the plan of economic mobilization. It is in some ways surprising that Jefferson Davis seems to have grasped this point, for in a message to Congress in November, 1864, he observed that slaves were sometimes treated as property, subject to impressment for short terms, but that "the slave . . . bears another relation to the state—that of a person. . . . In this [war] aspect, the relation of person predominates so far as to render it doubtful whether the private right of property can consistently and beneficially be continued and it would seem proper to acquire for the public service the entire property in the labor of the slave, and to pay therefor due compensation."

These failures, if failures they be—the failure to tax, the failure even to attempt an effective use of the cotton supply, the failure to achieve effective use of resources and manpower—all stemmed from attitudes which prevailed widely in the Confederacy. Insofar as they were errors, they were the errors of the South in general and not of the Confederate President nor any other one man in particular. In fact, the general level of political leadership in the Confederacy left much to be desired—as witness the parochialism of men like Governor Joseph E. Brown, who never really perceived that the defense of Georgia lay beyond the territorial boundaries of the state, or the negativism of men like Senator Henry S. Foote, whose futile ranting presented a painful anticlimax to the great tradition of Southern political excellence in the Federal Congress in the decades before the war.

But in appraising the part which political factors played in the failure of the Confederacy, it is necessary to look beyond the questions of formation of policy to the more human question of the quality of leadership. At this level, as distinguished from the policy level, there is a great deal of evidence to justify placing a considerable share of the responsibility for the Confederacy's misfortunes directly at the door of Jefferson Davis.

This is not at all the same thing as to say that the strictures of his critics were valid. In fact, the narrowness, pettiness, and lack of realism of men like Alexander Stephens, Brown, and Foote make the narrowness of Davis seem broad-gauge by comparison. Moreover, when these critics assailed him, they usually did so for the wrong reasons. Men who least understood what the South needed were the most vocal in attacking him, while the men who, like Lee and Benjamin, most clearly perceived his real shortcomings were the least vocal because they were also the ones who understood that whatever was to be accomplished must be accomplished through him. With his most acute critics always silent and his most obtuse ones never so, he enjoyed a brand of criticism which, however galling it may have been at the time, has helped his historical reputation, since history must vindicate him if he is measured by some of the accusations brought against him by his critics—accusations of despotism and too much centralization. But if he is measured, instead, by the tests which history itself would apply to the appraisal of leadership, what do we find? We find, it may be argued, a record of personal failure significant enough to have had a bearing on the course of the war.

Davis failed in three important ways—in his relations with other Confederate leaders and with the people, in his fundamental concept of his job as president, and in his specific handling of his politico-military role as commander in chief. In every one of these respects, Lincoln offered a striking contrast and presented superlative qualities of leadership.

Concerning Davis' relations with the Confederate leaders, Clifford Dowdey has remarked that he had only two first-rate minds among his advisers—Robert E. Lee and Judah P. Benjamin. Both men had to employ a disproportionate amount of their time and energy in exercising the supreme tact which was necessary in working with Davis. Benjamin was never permitted to bring his originality and resourcefulness into play, and he was forced to forfeit his influence with the public by silently accepting blame for measures which Davis chose not to explain to the people. As for Lee, he was held in peripheral commands or at a desk in Richmond until fourteen of the twenty-seven months during which the South still retained some striking power had passed. Davis never allowed him a post of overall command such as Winfield Scott, George B. McClellan, Henry W. Halleck, and U. S. Grant all enjoyed under Lincoln. When Congress adopted a bill establishing the office of general in chief, intended for Lee, Davis vetoed it.

Compare this record with that of Lincoln, who took both William H. Seward and Salmon Chase into his cabinet, who kept Charles Sumner on his side while at the same time holding border state moderates like Edward Bates, who formed a cabinet with four former Democrats and three former Whigs and blandly remarked that he could balance the elements since he was an old Whig himself. Compare, too, Lincoln's forebearance when Seward was trying to run the administration, Chase was conducting a presidential campaign against Lincoln from his post in the Treasury, and the Blair family was waging its bitter family feuds from the postmaster-general's office.

Again, it is revealing to compare Davis' attitude toward P. G. T. Beauregard when he felt that the Creole general was blaming him for the failure to reap the fruits of First Manassas, and Lincoln's attitude toward Joseph Hooker when he believed that Hooker was saying there ought to be a dictator at Washington. Davis wrote to Beauregard that he was "surprised" at that general's report of the battle "because if we did differ as to the measure and purposes of contemplated campaigns, such fact could have no appropriate place in the report of the battle; further, because it seemed to be an attempt to exalt yourself at my expense."[1]

The accusation was very likely valid, but Lincoln would not have made it. When he wrote to Hooker, it was to say: "I have heard, in such a way as to believe it, of your recently saying that both the army and the government needed a dictator. Of course it was not for this, but in spite of it, that I have given you the command. Only those generals who gain successes can set up dictators.

---

[1] It must be conceded that both Joseph E. Johnston and Beauregard gave Davis great provocation, and that he was sometimes astonishingly patient in replying to them, but he was also capable of being very starchy in his rebukes. When Brigadier General Whiting protested the policy of giving each brigade a commander from its own state, and declined the command of such a brigade himself, and when Johnston forwarded Whiting's letter to Richmond, Secretary Benjamin replied: "The President has read with grave displeasure the very insubordinate letter of General Whiting, in which he indulges in presumptuous censure of the orders of his commander-in-chief and tenders unasked advice to his superiors in command. . . . The President requests me to say that he trusts you will hereafter decline to forward to him communications of your subordinates having so obvious a tendency to excite a mutinous and disorganizing spirit in the army."

What I now ask of you is military success, and I will risk the dictatorship. The government will support you to the utmost of its ability, which is neither more nor less than it has done and will do for all commanders."

Just as Davis could not really work with other Confederate leaders, so also he could scarcely even communicate with the people of the Confederacy. He seemed to think in abstractions and to speak in platitudes. It is suggestive, I think, to recall his appeal to the men who had fought, suffered, lost their faith, and gone through hell under the command of Braxton Bragg and who wanted no more of their commanding general. Davis' way of dealing with these hard-bitten and badly demoralized soldiers was to praise in flowery language their virtues as fighting men and then, as a climax, to urge them: "Crown these [virtues] with harmony, due subordination, and cheerful support of lawful authority."

One reason for Davis' failure to communicate was that he could seldom admit he was wrong. He used an excessive share of his energy in contentious and even litigious argument to prove he was right. He seemed to feel that if he were right that was enough; that it was more important to vindicate his own rectitude than to get results. When a matter could not be explained without admitting a mistake, as for instance in the case of the loss of Roanoke Island, it simply did not get explained at all, and the people were alienated by the feeling that the administration dared not trust them with the truth. As a critic of Davis, Edward Pollard of the Richmond *Examiner* often displayed rank prejudice, but he came close to the truth when he said that Davis "has not told the people what he needed. As a faithful sentinel, he has not told them what of the night."

The contrast presented by Lincoln shows up clearly in a letter of Lincoln to Grant at the end of the Vicksburg campaign. "When you first reached the vicinity of Vicksburg," said Lincoln, "I never had any faith, except a general hope that you knew better than I, that the Yazoo Pass expedition, and the like, could succeed. When you got below, and took Port Gibson, Grand Gulf, and vicinity, I thought you should go down the river and join General [N. P.] Banks; and when you turned northward east of the Big Black, I feared it was a mistake. I now wish to make the personal acknowledgement that you were right and I was wrong."

This letter has no counterpart in the correspondence of Jefferson Davis.

If Davis failed in his relations with people, he failed also in his concept of his task as President. In April, 1861, history cast him in the role of a revolutionary leader. What such a role requires of a man is that he shall concentrate intensively upon the essentials, with a bold indifference to all that is irrelevant to the cause; that he shall hold to the level of overall leadership, leaving matters of detail to his subordinates; and that he shall have a driving instinct for success and a readiness to adopt the innovations which will bring success. Although Davis possessed talent and intelligence, it would have been hard to find a man more lacking in these qualifications than he.

Davis was a conservative leader, not a revolutionary leader; a man with a strong sense of protocol and convention, but with a weak sense of innovation; a man who was much happier with details than he was with overviews; a man who loved order and logical organization better than he loved results which are achieved by unorthodox methods; above all, a man who thought in terms of principles rather than of possibilities and who cared more about proving he was right than about gaining success.

All these qualities showed up in his handling of his duties as commander in chief. In that role, his other weaknesses were accentuated by his firm conviction that he possessed real military talent and that he should give his attention primarily to the close guidance of the operations of all the Confederate armies. Because of this conviction, he ran the war office himself and all six of his war secretaries were either nonentities or transients—even Benjamin seemingly exercised little initiative while in this post. For the same reason the giant, Lee, was never permitted to hold a general command such as even Halleck held under

Lincoln. The same irresistible temptation to run military operations himself also led Davis to descend to points of detail where he lost sight of the larger issues with which he should have concerned himself. Consequently, two of the severest criticisms of Davis have come from men who were in the War Department in Richmond. After serving Davis as secretary of war, George W. Randolph said that, despite all his attention to this area of activities, the President had "no practical knowledge of the workings of our military system in the field." Even more contemptuously, Robert G. H. Kean, an official of the department, said that Davis wasted time on "trash that ought to be dispatched by clerks."[2]

This attention to military detail resulted in something far more serious than the waste of presidential time. It meant that Davis made decisions in Richmond which should have been made in the field and that he hampered his field commanders by limiting their functions too narrowly and by interfering with their command. Not only did he sometimes visit battlefields and change the disposition of regiments while combat raged, but he sometimes sent orders to subordinate generals without consulting, and even without informing, their field commanders.[3]

A striking contrast to Davis' constant intervention appears in the policy of Lincoln, who was always concerned with military policy and often admonished his generals,

[2] On February 1, 1862, J. E. Johnston wrote to Benjamin: "I have been greatly surprised today to receive an order from the War Office detailing a private for a working party here. I hazard nothing in saying that in time of war, a Secretary of War never before made such a detail."

[3] On February 14, 1862, replying to a protest by J. E. Johnston, Davis said: "While I admit the propriety in all cases of transmitting orders through you to those under your command, it is not surprising that the Secretary of War should, in a case requiring prompt action, have departed from this usual method in view of the fact that he had failed more than once in having his instructions carried out when forwarded to you in the proper manner." This comes close to suggesting that, when a field commander is slow to obey orders, the proper remedy is to bypass him without informing him that he has been bypassed.

but who avoided details and refrained from giving orders. Lincoln's whole philosophy was expressed in a letter to Grant in 1864 in which he said, "The particulars of your plans, I neither know nor seek to know." By this statement Lincoln in no sense abdicated his authority as commander in chief. Rather, he clearly defined the true division of function between commander in chief and field commander. His role was to consider overall questions of military policy. The operational particulars were the business of the generals in the field. Lincoln knew this without learning it by experience. Davis never learned it despite his experience at West Point, in the Mexican War, and as secretary of war under Pierce.

If Davis had developed a military policy which would produce victory, his compulsion to run everything himself might not have mattered. But his decision to be his own secretary of war and his own general in chief meant that he was the author of Confederate military policy, and that he incorporated into this policy two fatal principles. One was the principle of departmentalization; the other, allied with it, was the principle of dispersion of force for the defense of territory, rather than concentration of force for the defeat of the enemy.

The principle of departmentalization appealed naturally to a man who thought in formal and static terms rather than in functional and dynamic ones. Like the dedicated bureaucrat that he was, Davis loved a symmetrical table of organization. Consequently, he did not hesitate to carry on the peacetime practice of assigning the units of the army to completely separate geographical departments, each one reporting solely to the war office and each operating independently of all the others. Sometimes this led to strange results. For instance, Lee, commanding in a department north of the James, and Beauregard, commanding in a department south of the James, converged in 1864 to defend Petersburg, but they continued to communicate with one another through the War Department in Richmond. But in fact, Lee and Beauregard did cooperate, despite the mechanical awkwardness of their situation. What was more serious was that, in general, the departmental commanders sought reinforcements for their own departments and looked to the defense of them without much regard for the needs of their fellows in other departments. One reason for the loss of Vicksburg was the fact that help had not come from the Trans-Mississippi Department, and Davis had rebuked Secretary Randolph for trying to bring help from that quarter. In June, 1863, Kean wrote: "The fatal notion of making each military department a separate nation for military purposes without subordination, co-operation, or concert—the same on which in point [of fact] the President and General Randolph split—has lost us Mississippi."[4] Dowdey, who also regards this departmentalization as one of the decisive factors in Confederate failure, remarks: "When Lee took over the War office, on hilly North Street, across from Capital Square [in 1862] Davis had a dispersal of forces in Virginia which, counting subdivisions of armies, had eight separate forces arranged in separate parts of the state. . . . The Confederate forces in Virginia were ready for anything except to fight a battle."

When accused of practicing dispersal, Davis denied that this was his policy, and he might have claimed, in extenuation, that the state governors exerted great pressure upon

---

[4] On July 12, Kean wrote further: "The radical vice of Mr. Davis's whole military system is the separate departmental organization, each reporting only to him. It makes each department depend only on its *own* strength and deprives them of the mutual support and combination which might else be obtained. It appears from a recent report of Richard Taylor that Vicksburg *might* have been relieved from that side; that the whole situation was treated with a levity incomprehensible when the vast stake is considered! Mr. Seddon remarked yesterday that he thought there was more blame on the command on the west than on the east side of the [Mississippi] river for its loss. It was a difference on this very principle of co-operation across the Mississippi, at this very point, Vicksburg, in connection with which General Randolph's resignation was brought about. His instruction to Holmes, who then had the command Smith now has, to cross over when necessary to produce the best results, and by virtue of his rank to take command of the combined force, was the thing of which the President so pointedly disapproved, and *countermanded*."

him to assign troops for local defense throughout many parts of the South. But he was committed to defensive action by temperament, if not by conviction. He never initiated the daring concentrations which Lee was willing to risk. He always thought in terms of repelling the invader rather than of smashing the enemy, and he was slow to recognize the fearful cost of defending fixed positions, as at Vicksburg. He never showed the compelling urgency of a man who knows that time is on the side of the enemy and that victory must be gained before the enemy's potential strength can be brought into play.

Once again the contrast with Lincoln is illuminating—and damaging to Davis. To my mind, it has been conclusively demonstrated that Lincoln had a sounder concept of the overall military objectives of the Union than any of his generals. He was impatient with the endless maneuvering and seeking of positional objectives which so completely dominated the thought of many of the generals, and he seldom lost sight of the ultimate goal of defeating the enemy's forces. T. Harry Williams quotes his message to Hooker: "I think Lee's Army, and not *Richmond,* is your true objective point. . . . Fight him when opportunity offers. If he stays where he is, fret him and fret him." Many months later, Lincoln wrote again, this time to General Halleck: "To avoid misunderstanding, let me say that to attempt to fight the enemy slowly back into his intrenchments at Richmond, and then to capture him, is an idea that I have been trying to repudiate for quite a year. . . . I have constantly desired the Army of the Potomac to make Lee's army and not Richmond, its objective point. If our army cannot fall upon the enemy and hurt him where he is, it is plain to me it can gain nothing by attempting to follow him over a succession of entrenched lines into a fortified city."

Many passages might be quoted to underscore the extent of the difference between Lincoln and Davis. But it would be hard to find any quotation which focuses the contrast quite as clearly as Lincoln's statement of what he liked about Ulysses S. Grant. I do not mean his curt:

"I can't spare this man; he fights," though that is apposite enough. What I am referring to is his observation: "General Grant is a copious worker and fighter but a very meager writer or telegrapher." If Davis was anything, he was a copious writer and telegrapher—so much so that Pollard said he had ink instead of blood in his veins—and what is more to the point, he seemed to cultivate this quality in his commanders. But he was a meager worker and fighter in terms of bringing about results, or even of clearly perceiving the results that needed to be brought about.

Fundamentally, Davis always thought in terms of what was right, rather than in terms of how to win. There is no real evidence in all the literature that Davis ever at any one time gave extended consideration to the basic question of what the South would have to do in order to win the war. He said almost nothing on this subject in his messages to Congress, which abounded in passages designed to prove the iniquity of the North and the rectitude of the South. By contrast, Lincoln wanted victory and wanted it so badly that in order to get it he was willing to co-operate with men who had shown they hated him. As he said, "I need success more than I need sympathy and I have not seen so much greater evidence of getting success from my sympathizers than from those who are denounced as the contrary." Lincoln thought of the war as something to be fought, but Davis thought of it as something to be conducted. There was no instinct for the jugular in Davis. That is why one seldom finds him pressing his generals to engage the enemy and never finds him striving for the concentration which might make possible a knockout blow.

In the light of Jefferson Davis' conspicuous lack of an instinct for victory, his lack of a drive and thrust for action and results, his failure to define his own office in terms of what needed to be accomplished, it hardly seems unrealistic to suppose that if the Union and the Confederacy had exchanged presidents with one another, the Confederacy might have won its independence. In this sense, is it not justifiable to doubt that the overwhelming statistical advantages of the North predestined the Confederacy to defeat? Historians have never developed a really satisfactory way of dealing with the relationship between the vast, impersonal, long-range social and economic forces of history and the immediate, close-range, somewhat accidental factors of personality; but here is certainly a case where the factors of personality played an important part in guiding the impact of the impersonal social and economic forces.

A political scientist might well object that it is superficial to emphasize these factors of personality without considering the question of what there was in the political system of the South that prevented the development of any viable alternative to the leadership of Davis. As we all know, any government may occasionally have the bad luck of putting an unsuitable man in a position of leadership. England, in 1939, had her Neville Chamberlain. No system can wholly prevent this from happening. But an effective political system, and especially an effective democratic system, is supposed to contain a mechanism which makes it possible to substitute new leadership when the existing leadership fails. England may have entered the Second World War with Chamberlain at the helm, but she ended with Winston Churchill dominating the scene. Granted there was no mute, inglorious Churchill waiting in the wings of the Confederacy, still there is abundant evidence that before the end of 1862 widespread and deep-seated dissatisfaction with Jefferson Davis was rife in the Confederacy. A great many people—perhaps the majority of informed men—knew that the choice of president had been a mistake. Yet there was no constructive opposition. The petulant, short-sighted, narrow-gauge, negativistic, vindictive quality of the criticisms of Davis made him seem, with all his shortcomings, a better man than most of those who assailed him. The Congress was little better than a bear garden, where Senator Benjamin Hill hit Senator William L. Yancey in the face with an inkwell, where a subordinate clerk of the House shot and killed the chief clerk on the capitol grounds, where a "lady" horsewhipped Senator George G. Vest, and where Senator Foote fought promiscuously with anyone who would fight him. Why did no legislative leader emerge to claim a legislative receivership for the bankrupt office of the executive?

This is a major question which suggests several lines of thought. For one thing, it tempts one to wonder to what extent the long years of defending slavery and building protective legalistic safeguards for the South as a minority section within the Union may have impaired the capacity for affirmative and imaginative action on the part of Southern leaders generally. How much had the vaunted statesmanship of the South suffered in this process? There is another suggestion which comes to mind. This is the possibility that the Confederacy may have suffered real and direct damage from the fact that its political organization lacked a two-party system. In the crisis of war, Southerners professed to regard it as a source of strength that they were not divided by party dissensions, but functionally a two-party system has important values. Where parties do not exist, criticism of the administration is likely to remain purely an individual matter; therefore the tone of the criticism is likely to be negative, carping, and petty, as it certainly was in the Confederacy. But where there are parties, the opposition group is strongly impelled to formulate real alternative policies and to press for the adoption of these policies on a constructive basis. In 1863 in the South, new Congressional elections were held, and, though history has neglected these elections most scandalously, we do know that they constituted a sharp rebuke to the administration and its followers.

Alternative leadership at that point, or even earlier, might have found a very substantial backing and might have been able to dominate policy. But the absence of a two-party system meant the absence of any available alternative leadership, and the protest votes which were cast in the election became mere expressions of futile and frustrated dissatisfaction rather than implements of a decision to adopt new and different policies for the Confederacy. Thus, the political leadership could not be altered, and Jefferson Davis continued to the end in his distinctive role—not a role which destiny fatalistically forced upon him, but one for which his qualities and temperament peculiarly fitted him and which he fulfilled in a very functional sense—the role of the leader of a Lost Cause.

For Further Reading

Studies devoted primarily to explaining the reasons for Northern victory in the Civil War are not numerous. Among the most interesting are Robert Tansill, *A Free and Impartial Exposition of the Causes Which Led to the Failure of the Confederate States to Establish Their Independence* (Washington, 1865, a rare pamphlet in the Clarendon MSS, Bodleian Library, Oxford University); Albert Bushnell Hart, "Why the South was Defeated in the Civil War," *New England Magazine,* V (new series, 1891); Duncan Ross, "Why the Confederacy Failed," *Century Magazine,* LIII (1896); Lawrence Henry Gipson, "The Collapse of the Confederacy," *Mississippi Valley Historical Review,* IV (1918); Charles H. Wesley, *The Collapse of the Confederacy* (Washington, 1937); Charles W. Ramsdell, *Behind the Lines in the Southern Confederacy* (Baton Rouge, 1944); and Bell Irvin Wiley, *The Road to Appomattox* (Memphis, 1956).

Of course, every general history of the Civil War period contains, either explicitly or implicitly, some judgments on the reasons for Southern defeat. Some basic interpretations are: John W. Burgess, *The Civil War and the Constitution, 1859–1865* (New York, 1901); James Ford Rhodes, *Lectures on the American Civil War* (New York, 1913) and *History of the Civil War, 1861–1865* (New York, 1917); Edward Channing, *The War for Southern Independence (A History of the United States,* Vol. 4 [New York, 1925]); A. C. Cole, *The Irrepressible Conflict, 1850–1865* (New York, 1934); Carl Russell Fish, *The American Civil War: An Interpretation* (London, New York, 1937); George Fort Milton, *Conflict: The American Civil War* (New York, 1941); J. G. Randall, *The Civil War and Reconstruction* (Boston, 1953); Allan Nevins, *The Statesmanship of the Civil War* (New York, 1953) and *The War for the Union: The Improvised War, 1861–1862* (New York, 1959); and Bruce Catton, *This Hallowed Ground* (New York, 1956).

The best general histories of the Confederacy are Ellis Merton Coulter, *The Confederate States of America, 1861–1865* (Baton Rouge, 1950); Clement Eaton, *A History of the Southern Confederacy* (New York, 1954); and Clifford Dowdey, *The Land They Fought For: The South as the Confederacy, 1832–1865* (New York, 1955).

The many economic difficulties which confronted the Confederacy are well analyzed in John Christopher Schwab, *The Confederate States of America, 1861–1865: A Financial and Industrial History* (New York, 1901); Robert C. Black, III, *The Railroads of the Confederacy* (Chapel Hill, 1952); Richard C. Todd, *Confederate Finance* (Athens, Ga., 1954); and Ella Lonn, *Salt as a Factor in the Confederacy* (New York, 1933). Important articles are Eugene Lerner, "The Monetary and Fiscal Programs of the Confederate Government, 1861–1865," *Journal of Political Economy*, LXII (1954), and "Money, Prices, and Wages in the Confederacy, 1861–1865," *ibid.*, LXIII (1955).

Jefferson Davis has been a source of much controversy among historians. His own *Rise and Fall of the Confederate Government* (2 vols., New York, 1881) is revealing, not merely for what it includes, but for what it neglects. Dunbar Rowland compiled his correspondence and public papers in *Jefferson Davis, Constitutionalist* (10 vols., Jackson, Miss., 1923). Edward A. Pollard, his bitter critic, wrote a harshly adverse *Life of Jefferson Davis, with a Secret History of the Southern Confederacy* (Philadelphia, Chicago, St. Louis, Atlanta, 1869); and his wife, Varina Howell Davis, presented what is perhaps the most convincing favorable portrayal yet to appear in her *Jefferson Davis, Ex-President of the Confederate States of America, a Memoir by his Wife* (2 vols., New York, 1890). Twentieth-century biographers have been rather favorable and not very searching in their appraisals. The most recent and most laudatory of these is Hudson Strode, *Jefferson Davis* (2 vols. to the year 1864; New York, 1955, 1959). The reader is likely to find more actual insight into Davis' policies as war president in Burton J. Hendrick, *Statesmen* of the Lost Cause: Jefferson Davis and His Cabinet (Boston, 1939); and Rembert W. Patrick, *Jefferson Davis and His Cabinet* (Baton Rouge, 1944). James Z. Rabun, "Alexander H. Stephens and Jefferson Davis," *American Historical Review*, LVIII (1953), is an important study of Davis' principal critic. Two diaries kept by minor officials in the Confederate War Department afford remarkable insights into the operations of the Davis administration: John Beauchamp Jones, *A Rebel War Clerk's Diary* (2 vols., Philadelphia, 1866); and Edward Younger (ed.), *Inside the Confederate Government: The Diary of Robert Garlick Hill Kean* (New York, 1957).

A full political history of the Confederacy has yet to be written. Albert Burton Moore, *Conscription and Conflict in the Confederacy* (New York, 1924), gives a good general account of local opposition to Davis' policies. For the Vance-Holden contest, see Richard E. Yates, *The Confederacy and Zeb Vance* (Tuscaloosa, 1958). On affairs in Georgia, Louise Biles Hill, *Governor Joseph E. Brown and the Confederacy* (Chapel Hill, 1939) and T. Conn Bryan, *Confederate Georgia* (Athens, Ga., 1953) are excellent. Also outstanding are Charles Edward Cauthen, *South Carolina Goes to War, 1861–1865* (Chapel Hill, 1950); John K. Bettersworth, *Confederate Mississippi* (Baton Rouge, 1943); and Jefferson Davis Bragg, *Louisiana in the Confederacy* (Baton Rouge, 1941). William M. Robinson, Jr., *Justice in Grey* (Cambridge, 1941) is an exhaustive treatment of Confederate judicial and constitutional problems.

The social and economic problems confronting the Union government have not been thoroughly explored by recent scholars. The best general discussion is still Emerson D. Fite, *Social and Industrial Conditions in the North during the Civil War* (New York, 1910). Wesley C. Mitchell, *A History of the Greenbacks* (Chicago, 1903) remains the standard work. See also Milton Friedman, "Price, Income and Monetary Changes in Three Wartime Periods," *American Economic Review*, LXII (1952); and Marshall A. Robinson, "Federal Debt Management: Civil

War, World War I and World War II," *ibid.*, XLV (1955).

The literature on Lincoln is vast. The best guides to it are Jay Monaghan (ed.), *Lincoln Bibliography, 1839–1939* (2 vols., Springfield, 1945); Paul McClelland Angle, *A Shelf of Lincoln Books* (New Brunswick, N.J., 1946); and Ralph Newman, "Basic Lincolniana," *Civil War History*, III (1957). The definitive compilation of Lincoln's writings is Roy P. Basler (ed.), *The Collected Works of Abraham Lincoln* (9 vols., New Brunswick, N.J., 1953–55). The best one-volume biography is Benjamin P. Thomas, *Abraham Lincoln* (New York, 1952); and the most satisfactory full-length study is J. G. Randall and Richard N. Current, *Lincoln the President* (4 vols., New York, 1945–55). Recent writers have stressed Lincoln's political sagacity: Harry J. Carman and Reinhard H. Luthin, *Lincoln and the Patronage* (New York, 1943); David Donald, *Lincoln Reconsidered* (New York, 1956); Burton J. Hendrick, *Lincoln's War Cabinet* (Boston, 1946); William B. Hesseltine, *Lincoln and the War Governors* (New York, 1948); Richard Hofstadter, "Abraham Lincoln and the Self-Made Myth," in his *The American Political Tradition* (New York, 1948); T. Harry Williams, "Abraham Lincoln: Principle and Pragmatism in Politics," *Mississippi Valley Historical Review*, XL (1953); and William Frank Zornow, *Lincoln and the Party Divided* (Norman, Okla., 1954).

New studies of most of the Northern states during the Civil War period are badly needed. Of the existing books Frederick Merk, *Economic History of Wisconsin during the Civil War Decade* (Madison, 1916) and Arthur C. Cole, *The Era of the Civil War, 1848–1870 (The Centennial History of Illinois,* Vol. 3 [Springfield, 1919]) are the most useful. Kenneth M. Stampp, *Indiana Politics during the Civil War* (Indianapolis, 1949) is an incisive and provocative work.

On civil rights in the North, the standard work is J. G. Randall, *Constitutional Problems under Lincoln* (Urbana, Ill., 1951). See Robert S. Harper, *Lincoln and the Press*

(New York, 1951) for editorial attacks on Lincoln, and J. G. Randall, "The Unpopular Mr. Lincoln," *Lincoln the Liberal Statesman* (New York, 1947) for other contemporary criticisms.

The literature on Civil War military history is massive, but little of it gives attention to the cultural and intellectual forces that shaped the generalship of the war. David Donald's "Refighting the Civil War," *Lincoln Reconsidered,* is an attempt to explore the influences of Jomini upon Confederate and Union strategy. A perceptive essay on Jomini appears in Edward M. Earle (ed.), *Makers of Modern Strategy* (Princeton, 1944), Chapter 4, "Jomini," by Crane Brinton, Gordon A. Craig, and Felix Gilbert. Jomini and his background are also treated in R. S. Preston, S. F. Wise, and H. O. Werner, *Men in Arms* (New York, 1956). The best source for Jomini's thought is his own writings: J. D. Hittle (ed.), *Jomini and His Summary of the Art of War* (Harrisburg, 1947). For a convenient introduction to other writers on the art of war see Thomas R. Phillips (ed.), *Roots of Strategy* (London, 1943). Valuable secondary treatments are Cyril Falls, *A Hundred Years of War* (London, 1953); and F. E. Adcock, *The Greek and Macedonian Art of War* (Berkeley, Calif., 1957), especially Chapter 6, "Generalship in Battle."

Civil War high command and strategy are treated in E. W. Sheppard, "Policy and Command in the American Civil War," *The Army Quarterly,* XXXVI (1939); Sir Frederick Maurice, *Statesmen and Soldiers of the Civil War* (Boston, 1926); and T. Harry Williams, *Lincoln and His Generals* (New York, 1952). Frank E. Vandiver dissects the Confederate military hierarchy in *Rebel Brass: The Confederate Command System* (Baton Rouge, 1956). Particularly good for its discussion of the three greatest military figures of the war is A. H. Burne, *Lee, Grant, and Sherman* (New York, 1939). The best analysis of Grant's generalship, which sometimes turns into a too ardent defense, is J. F. C. Fuller, *The Generalship of Ulysses S. Grant* (London, 1929), and *Grant and Lee* (London,

1933). Also good on Grant are C. F. Atkinson, *Grant's Campaigns of 1864 and 1865* (London, 1908); A. L. Conger, *The Rise of U. S. Grant* (New York, 1931); and Kenneth P. Williams, *Lincoln Finds a General* (5 vols., New York, 1949–59). In *Sherman* (New York, 1929), B. H. Liddell Hart explores Sherman's development from a Jominian to a prophet of total war, in the process finding support for his own strategic doctrine. Douglas S. Freeman details Lee's military career in *Robert E. Lee: A Biography* (4 vols., New York, 1934–35) and evaluates his subject's generalship in Chapter 11, Volume IV, "The Sword of Robert E. Lee."

On the common soldier in the Civil War the outstanding works are Bell Irvin Wiley, *The Life of Johnny Reb* (Indianapolis, New York, 1943), and *The Life of Billy Yank* (Indianapolis, 1951), both distinguished for thorough research and careful analysis. David Donald discusses democratic tendencies in the Southern army in "The Confederate as a Fighting Man," *Journal of Southern History,* XXV (1959). On the Federal army the standard work is Fred A. Shannon, *The Organization and Administration of the Union Army, 1861–1865* (2 vols., Cleveland, 1928). Jack Franklin Leach, *Conscription in the United States: Historical Background* (Rutland, Vt., 1952) is valuable. Dudley Taylor Cornish, *The Sable Arm* (New York, 1956), is the best study of Negro troops in the Union Army. Ella Lonn has fully discussed the role of Europeans in the Civil War in *Foreigners in the Confederacy* (Chapel Hill, 1940) and *Foreigners in the Union Army and Navy* (Baton Rouge, 1951).

There are two standard works on Europe's relationship to the American Civil War. E. D. Adams, *Great Britain and the American Civil War* (2 vols., London, 1925) is a detailed and scholarly study of the British position, whereas F. L. Owsley has analyzed the Southern effort to secure recognition in his *King Cotton Diplomacy* (Chicago, 1931). Concerned with European opinion toward the American struggle are D. Jordan and E. J. Pratt, *Europe and the American Civil War* (Boston, 1931); L. M. Case (ed.), *French Opinion on the United States and Mexico, 1860–1867* (New York, 1936); and W. R. West, *Contemporary French Opinion on the American Civil War* (Baltimore, 1924). Enlightening articles on various segments of British attitudes are W. D. Jones, "The British Conservatives and the American Civil War," *American Historical Review,* LVIII (1953); J. H. Park, "The English Workingmen and the American Civil War," *Political Science Quarterly,* XXXIX (1924); and M. P. Claussen, "Peace Factors in Anglo-American Relations, 1861–1863," *Mississippi Valley Historical Review, XXVI* (1940).

Much has been written on the maritime issues raised by the Civil War. On the *Trent* affair are C. F. Adams, Jr., "The Trent Affair," *Massachusetts Historical Society Proceedings,* XLV (1911); Thomas Harris, *The Trent Affair* (Indianapolis, 1896); V. H. Cohen, "Charles Sumner and the *Trent* Affair," *Journal of Southern History,* XXII (1956); and W. W. Jeffries, "The Civil War Career of Charles Wilkes," *Journal of Southern History,* XI (1945). On questions of neutral rights and freedom of the seas, see F. L. Owsley, "America and the Freedom of the Seas, 1861–1865," in Avery Craven (ed.), *Essays in Honor of William E. Dodd* (Chicago, 1935); J. P. Baxter, "The British Government and Neutral Rights, 1861–1865," *American Historical Review,* XXXIV (1928) and "Some British Opinions as to Neutral Rights, 1861–1865," *American Journal of International Law,* XXIII (1929); and D. H. Maynard's two articles, "Union Efforts to Prevent the Escape of the *Alabama,*" *Mississippi Valley Historical Review,* XLI (1954) and "Plotting the Escape of the *Alabama,*" *Journal of Southern History,* XX (1954).

Perhaps the best analysis of Seward's leadership can be found in Samuel F. Bemis (ed.), *The American Secretaries of State and Their Diplomacy* (New York, 1925), VII. Another useful survey is Frederic Bancroft, *The Life of William H. Seward* (New York, 1900), II. For Lincoln's role see Jay Monaghan, *Diplomat in Carpet Slippers* (Indianapolis, 1945). On Adams in London, see W. C. Ford (ed.), *A Cycle of Adams Letters, 1861–1865* (2 vols., Boston, 1920) and the fascinating journal of one member of the legation, S. A. Wallace and F. E. Gillespie (eds.), *The Journal of Benjamin Moran, 1857–1865* (2 vols., Chicago, 1949). On another American diplomat of the period see Margaret Clapp, *Forgotten First Citizen: John Bigelow* (Boston, 1947). For a good evaluation of two British diplomats see Lord Newton, *Lord Lyons* (2 vols., London, 1913) and Spencer Walpole, *Life of Lord John Russell* (2 vols., London, 1891). On Slidell's fruitless mission to Paris, see L. M. Sears, "A Confederate Diplomat at the Court of Napoleon III," *American Historical Review,* XXVI (1931). W. H. Russell, *My Diary North and South* (2 vols., London, 1863) is an interesting analysis of wartime diplomacy from the viewpoint of a leading British correspondent.

Index

Lerner, Eugene M., 22
Liddell Hart, B. H., 52
Lincoln, Abraham, on Northern wartime growth, 30–1; and McClellan, 45–6; and McClernand, 51; as strategist, 53–4, 108–9; ignores Seward's plan for foreign war, 58; modifies Seward's belligerent dispatch, 61; suspends writ of habeas corpus, 86–7; abused by Northern press, 87; intervenes in Northern elections, 88–90; succeeds in relations with political rivals, 101–2; as commander in chief, 105–6
Lindsay, William S., 67
Longstreet, James, 24, 43, 80–1
Lonn, Ella, 24
Lynchburg *Virginian,* 16
Lyons, Lord, 58, 59, 62, 68

McClellan, George B., 36, 49; admires Jomini, 40; appraised as a general, 42, 44–5; retires from before Richmond, 66–7; defeated, 68
McClernand, John A., 51
Mahan, Dennis Hart, 41, 46
Mahone, William, 49
Mason, James M., 63–4, 69, 75
Meade, George G., 36, 42, 44–5
Memminger, Christopher G., cotton policy of, 19–21; appraised as a financier, 22–3; compared with Chase, 25; disapproves cotton embargo, 95
Mercier, Henri, 57, 62, 68, 73–74
Monroe, James, 77
Morton, O. P., 89
Motley, John L., 69

Napoleon I, 34, 35, 38
Napoleon III, 57, 67–8, 72. *See also* France
Negroes, as factor in Union armies, 83; Confederate failure to conscript, 98–9
Northrop, Lucius B., 95

Owsley, Frank L., 20, 22

Palmerston, Lord, contemplates British intervention in American Civil War, 70; urges delay in recognition of Confederacy, 71; opposes mediation 72; accepts British position as looker-on at war, 77; unmoved by sentiment, 78
Patrick, Rembert W., 20–1
Pemberton, John C., 36
Political leadership, as factor in Confederate defeat, 91–112
Political parties, absence of, as factor in Confederate defeat, 111
Pollard, Edward A., on failure of the South, 16, 17, 18; condemns Southern cotton policy, 19; quoted, 25; attacks Davis, 84, 103, 109

Railroads, as a factor in Confederate defeat, 24, 27, 30
Ramsdell, C. W., 25, 26, 31
Randolph, George W., 85, 96, 105, 107
Richmond *Examiner,* 19
Rosecrans, William S., 36, 42, 45
Russell, Lord John, concerned over Seward's policies, 59; fails to recognize Confederate emissaries, 61–2; declines English mediation in American Civil War, 62; on *Treat* affair, 64; refuses to recognize Confederacy, 69–70; fails to fight for Confederate recognition, 72–3; gives Britain's final refusal to intervene, 75
Russell, William H., 62
Russia, and American Civil War, 57–8, 73

Saxe, Marshal, 34, 35, 40
Schwab, John C., 22
Scott, Winfield, 37
Seddon, J. A., 82
Seward, William H., formulates